Iraq's Military Capabilities in 2002

Other Books by Anthony H. Cordesman

The Lessons of Afghanistan: War Fighting, Intelligence, and Force Transformation (CSIS, 2002)

Cyberthreats, Information Warfare, and Critical Infrastructure Protection: Defending the U.S. Homeland, with Justin Cordesman (Praeger/CSIS, 2002)

Strategic Threats and National Missile Defenses: Defending the U.S. Homeland (Praeger/CSIS, 2002)

Terrorism, Asymmetric Warfare, and Weapons of Mass Destruction: Defending the U.S. Homeland (Praeger/CSIS, 2002)

A Tragedy of Arms: Military and Security Developments in the Maghreb (Praeger, 2001)

Peace and War: The Arab-Israeli Military Balance Enters the 21st Century (Praeger, 2001)

The Lessons and Non-Lessons of the Air and Missile Campaign in Kosovo (Praeger, 2000)

Iran in Transition: Conventional Threats and Weapons of Mass Destruction (Praeger, 1999)

Iraq and the War of the Sanctions: Conventional Threats and Weapons of Mass Destruction (Praeger, 1999)

Transnational Threats from the Middle East (U.S. Army War College, 1999)

Bahrain, Oman, Qatar, and the UAE: Challenges of Security (Westview/CSIS, 1997)

Iran: Dilemmas of Dual Containment, with Ahmed Hashim (Westview/CSIS, 1997)

Iraq: Sanctions and Beyond, with Ahmed Hashim (Westview/CSIS, 1997)

Kuwait: Recovery and Security after the Gulf War (Westview/CSIS, 1997)

Saudi Arabia: Guarding the Desert Kingdom (Westview/CSIS, 1997)

U.S. Forces in the Middle East: Resources and Capabilities (Westview/CSIS, 1997)

Perilous Prospects: The Peace Process and Arab-Israeli Military Balance (Westview, 1996)

Iran and Iraq: The Threat from the Northern Gulf (Westview, 1994)

After the Storm: The Changing Military Balance in the Middle East (Westview, 1993)

Weapons of Mass Destruction in the Middle East (Brassey's, 1991)

The Lessons of Modern War (4 vols.), with Abraham R. Wagner (Westview, 1990–1995)

The Gulf and the West (Westview, 1988)

NATO's Central Region Forces (Jane's, 1988)

The Iran-Iraq War and Western Security, 1984–1987 (Jane's, 1987)

The Arab-Israeli Balance and the Art of Operations (AEI, 1987)

Western Strategic Interests and Saudi Arabia (Croom Helm, 1987)

The Gulf and the Search for Strategic Stability (Westview, 1984)

Jordanian Arms and the Middle East Balance (Middle East Institute, 1983)

Iraq's Military Capabilities in 2002
A Dynamic Net Assessment

Author
Anthony H. Cordesman

September 2002

About CSIS

For four decades, the Center for Strategic and International Studies (CSIS) has been dedicated to providing world leaders with strategic insights on—and policy solutions to—current and emerging global issues.

CSIS is led by John J. Hamre, former U.S. deputy secretary of defense. It is guided by a board of trustees chaired by former U.S. senator Sam Nunn and consisting of prominent individuals from both the public and private sectors.

The CSIS staff of 190 researchers and support staff focus primarily on three subject areas. First, CSIS addresses the full spectrum of new challenges to national and international security. Second, it maintains resident experts on all of the world's major geographical regions. Third, it is committed to helping to develop new methods of governance for the global age; to this end, CSIS has programs on technology and public policy, international trade and finance, and energy.

Headquartered in Washington, D.C., CSIS is private, bipartisan, and tax-exempt. CSIS does not take specific policy positions; accordingly, all views expressed herein should be understood to be solely those of the author.

Cover Photo Credit
Crossed Swords Triumphal Arch (Baghdad)
© Shepard Sherbell/CORBIS SABA

Library of Congress Cataloging-in-Publication Data
Cordesman, Anthony H.
    Iraq's military capabilities in 2002 : a dynamic net assessment /Anthony H. Cordesman.
        p. cm.—(CSIS Report)
    Includes bibliographical references.
    ISBN 0-89206-416-1
    1. Iraq—Armed Forces. 2. Iraq—Defenses. 3. Iraq—Military policy. 4. United States—Military policy. I. Title.
    UA853.I75 C653 2002
    355'.0332567'090511—dc21   2002012857

The CSIS Press
Center for Strategic and International Studies
1800 K Street, N.W., Washington, D.C. 20006
Telephone: (202) 887-0200
Fax: (202) 775-3199
E-mail: books@csis.org
Web site: http://www.csis.org/

Contents

Acknowledgments

This document is an expanded version of a report originally prepared for a conference at the Naval War College in July 2002. The author would like to thank his colleagues at that conference for many suggestions and corrections. He would also like to thank the Smith Richardson Foundation for some of the funding for the project.

Introduction

Any effort to provide a dynamic net assessment of Iraq's military capabilities in various war-fighting contingencies involves a wide range of challenges. The uncertainties and intangibles affecting any assessment of Iraq's military capabilities—and any war that has not yet been fought—are at least as important as the hard data on its force strength and order of battle.

There is reason for modesty in any form of military analysis and above all in speculating about future wars. The proper rules for such analysis were laid out more than two millennia ago by Thucydides in writing his *History of the Peloponnesian War* (c. 420 B.C.): "I did not even trust my own impressions, but it rests partly on what I saw myself, partly on what others saw for me, the accuracy of the report being always tried by the most severe and detailed tests possible." These are tests no one can meet in talking about a war that has not happened, and in this case there are many options and possible contingencies.

Iraq is already involved in a political struggle against the United States and its neighbors that is an extension of war by other means, and the course of this "war of sanctions" can sharply alter Iraq's military capabilities over time. Although current attention focuses on U.S. military efforts to overthrow Saddam Hussein's regime, Iraq may become involved in a wide range of conflicts, many of which may take on a number of different forms and become asymmetric in character. Iraq's continuing efforts to develop weapons of mass destruction and advanced delivery systems compound both the uncertainties in assessing its military capabilities and the uncertainties as to how it would behave in given contingencies.

Nevertheless, a great deal is known about Iraq's military capabilities and probable behavior as well as about the military capabilities and behavior of its potential enemies. The list of potential contingencies is limited, and there are often severe constraints on the options available to Iraq and its opponents. As a result, it is possible to make educated "guesstimates" on Iraq's capabilities relative to most key scenarios and about the strengths and weaknesses of its position in most contingencies.

Iraq's Current Military Forces

The Iraqi Army and Key Security Elements

It is relatively easy to estimate the total size of Iraqi military forces and to comment in broad terms on their capabilities. Although Iraq's forces have many serious defects, Iraq remains the most effective military power in the Gulf, despite the Gulf War and the loss of some 40 percent of its army and air force order of battle. Iraq still has armed forces of around 424,000 men and an inventory of some 2,200 main battle tanks, 3,700 other armored vehicles, and 2,400 major artillery weapons. It also has more than 300 combat aircraft with potential operational status.[1] As weak as many aspects of Iraq's forces may be, it is a major military power by regional standards and has at least some chemical and biological weapons. Iraq must be taken seriously both in regional terms and in any military effort to overthrow the regime of Saddam Hussein.

Strength

Iraqi forces are under the command of loyalists to the regime. These include General Sultan Hashim al-Ubaydi, the minister of defense, and General Ibrahim Abd Al-Satter Muhammad al-Tikriti, the chief of staff. The International Institute of Strategic Studies (IISS) estimates that the Iraqi army still can deploy some 375,000 men, organized into 7 corps, with 2 Republican Guard corps and 5 regular army corps. These forces include 6 Republican Guard divisions (3 armored, 1 mechanized, and 2 infantry) plus 4 Special Republican Guard brigades. The regular army has some 16 divisions, and although 11 are relatively low-grade infantry divisions, 3 are armored divisions and 3 are mechanized divisions. The regular army also has 5 commando and 2 special forces brigades.

Other estimates by U.S. Central Command (USCENTCOM) indicate that the Iraqi land forces have a total strength of 700,000 personnel, including reserves. These estimates indicate that Iraq's major combat formations include 17 regular army divisions (6 heavy and 11 light) and 6 Republican Guard divisions (3 heavy and 3 light). USCENTCOM also estimates that the total Iraqi army order of battle includes 6 armored divisions, 4 mechanized divisions, 10 infantry divisions, 2 special forces divisions, 1 Special Republican Guard or Presidential Guard division, 19 reserve brigades, 15 People's Army brigades, and 25 helicopter squadrons.[2]

---

1. These Iraqi force estimates are based largely upon Anthony H. Cordesman, *Iraq and the War of Sanctions* (Westport: Praeger, 1999); the International Institute for Strategic Studies (IISS), *The Military Balance, 2001–2002* (London: Oxford University Press for the IISS, 2001), and material in the Internet edition of *Jane's Sentinel Security Assessments*, accessed in June 2002.

Although these units lack modern training and the regular army units heavily depend on conscripts, more than one third are full-time regulars or long-service reservists. U.S. experts estimate that Iraqi divisions differ significantly by unit, but have an average authorized strength of about 10,000 men, and that about half of the 23 Iraqi divisions have manning levels of around 8,000 men and "a fair state of readiness." Although at least half of the regular army has manning levels of about 70 percent of authorized strength or lower and some infantry units have very poor manning levels and heavily depend on Shi'ite, Kurdish, and Turkoman conscripts, Republican Guard divisions have an average authorized strength of around 8,000 to 10,000 men and seem to average at least 80 percent of authorized strength. Brigades average around 2,500 men—the size of a large U.S. battalion.[3] Both sets of estimates give Iraq a total force, today, of approximately 20–23 division equivalents, versus 35–40 division equivalents in the summer of 1990, and 67–70 division equivalents in January 1991—just before the Coalition offensives began in the Gulf War.[4] Iraqi manning levels are, however, uncertain. There are many reports of badly under-manned units, but Iraq has also carried out a number of reserve call-ups in 2002.[5]

The Iraqi army relies on large numbers of combat-worn and obsolescent weapons, but it does have some 700 relatively modern T-72 tanks, 900 BMP-series armored infantry fighting vehicles (AIFVs), 150 self-propelled artillery weapons, and 200 multiple rocket launchers. It has extensive stocks of AT-3, AT-4, Milan, and High-subsonic Optically Teleguided (HOT) anti-tank guided weapons, and roughly 100 attack and 275 utility/transport helicopters. The mobile elements of Iraq's 17,000 man Air Defense Command can deploy large numbers of manportable surface-to-air missiles, plus SA-7, SA-8, SA-9, and Roland vehicle-mounted surface-to-air missiles. Iraqi logistics are weak, subject to political controls to prevent coup attempts, and limited by sanctions that have prevented most arms imports for more than a decade. Iraqi combat engineering and bridging, however, are good.

Iraq also has extensive internal security and paramilitary forces. The entire police and law enforcement system performs internal security functions, and there are parallel internal security services with units in virtually every town and city. The Republican Guard and Special Republican Guard units are specially trained for urban warfare and security operations, as well as conventional military operations, and there are three paramilitary forces. The security troops have some 15,000 men, the border guards around 9,000, and Saddam's Fedayeen consists of 18,000 to 20,000 men.

Deployment

U.S. experts indicate that Iraq's divisions were arrayed north to south in early 2001, with a mix of regular and Republican Guard divisions. All of the divisions near the Kuwait border are regular, although some Republican Guard divisions could move

---

2. Estimates provided by USCENTCOM in June 1996 and 1997, plus interviews.
3. USCENTCOM briefing by "senior military official.
4. Estimate first provided by USCENTCOM in June 1996 plus interviews.
5. *London Daily Telegraph*, July 19, 2002, p. 1.

to the border relatively rapidly. U.S. experts indicate that Iraqi land forces have a total of 14 divisions in the north, 3 divisions in central Iraq, and 6 divisions south of An Najaf. The Republican Guard had a total of 3 armored divisions deployed in the vicinity of Baghdad—1 near Taji, 1 near Baghdad, and 1 near As Suwayrah.[6] All Republican Guard divisions are located above the 32-degree line. Several additional Republican Guard divisions are located around Baghdad to play a major role in internal security. Several more Republican Guard divisions were located north of Baghdad closer to the Kurdish area.[7]

Estimates by Jane's indicate that the regular army is organized into five major corps, with 17 main force division equivalents and major bases at Baghdad, Basra, Kirkuk, and Mosul. There are major training areas west of Baghdad, near Mosul, and in the marsh areas in the south. The training area southwest of Basra has had only limited use because of the "no-fly zones."[8]

If one exempts the forces dedicated to the security of the regime and deployed near Baghdad and similar internal security garrisons in Basra and Kirkuk, the army forces are deployed as follows:

- *Northern Iraq*: The 1st Corps is headquartered at Kirkuk and the 5th Corps at Mosul. They guard the Turkish border area, deploy on the edge of the Kurdish enclave, and protect the oil fields in the north.

  - The 1st Corps includes the 2nd Infantry Division headquartered at Alrabee, the 5th Mechanized Division headquartered at Shuwan, the 8th Infantry Division headquartered at Shuwan, and the 38th Infantry Division headquartered at Quader Karam.

  - The 5th Corps has units defending the border area with Syria. It includes the 1st Mechanized Division headquartered at Makhmur, the 4th Infantry Division headquartered at Bashiqa Maonten, the 7th Infantry Division headquartered at Alton Kopri Castle, and the 16th Infantry Division headquartered near the Saddam Dam and Mosul.

- *Eastern Iraq*: The 2nd Corps is headquartered at Deyala and is deployed east of Baghdad to defend against Iran or any attack by Iranian-backed Iraqi opposition forces. It includes the 3rd Armored Division headquartered at Jalawia, the 15th Infantry Division headquartered at Amerli, and the 34th Infantry Division headquartered near Khanaqin.

- *Southern Iraq* has two corps that play a major role in securing Shi'ite areas and suppressing Shi'ite dissidents.

  - The 3rd Corps is headquartered in the Nasseria area and is positioned near the Kuwaiti border. It includes the 6th Armored Division headquartered near Majnoon and Al Nashwa, the 11th Infantry Division headquartered at Al Naserria, and the 51st Mechanized Division headquartered at Zubair.

---

6. Based on interviews.
7. USCENTCOM briefing by "senior military official."
8. *Jane's Sentinel Security Assessments,* "Iraqi Army," online edition, accessed May 7, 2002.

- The 4th corps is headquartered at Al Amara and defends the border with Iran. It includes the 10th Armored Division headquartered near Al Teab and Al Amara, the 14th Infantry Division headquartered south of Al Amara, and the 18th Infantry Division headquartered near Al Amara and Al Musharah.

The Republican Guard adds two more corps, with seven divisions, to this list:

■ *The Northern Corps of the Republican Guard* can act to defend against Iran and operate against the Kurds, but its primary mission seems to be the defense of the greater Baghdad area and Tikrit. The Al Madina Al Munawara Armored Division, with four brigades, is located at the Al Rashedia and Al Taji camps and plays a key role in defending the outer Baghdad area. The Special Republican Guard provides protection and defense within the city. The Northern Corps also includes the 1st Adnan Mechanized Division at Mosul, the 2nd Baghdad Infantry Division at Maqloob Maontin-Mosul, and the Al Abed Infantry Division at Kirkuk-Khalid Camp.

■ *The Southern Corps of the Republican Guard* is headquartered at Al Hafreia and the Al Fateh al Mubin Command Center. It helps defend against Iran in the south, as well as any U.S.-led attack, and acts as a deterrent force to suppress any Shi'ite uprising. Its forces include the Nabu Khuth Nusser Infantry Division at Al Husseinia-al Kutt, the Hamurabi Mechanized Division in the Al Wahda area, and the Al Nedaa Armored Division near Baaquba-Deyla.

The Special Republican Guard adds 4 brigades, which are located largely within Baghdad and are organized to defend the regime. The Special Republican Guard has 4 infantry/motorized brigades with 14 battalions, an armored brigade, and an air defense command with elements to secure Baghdad's ground-based air defenses against any coup attempt. It has a total active strength of about 12,000 to 15,000, but can rapidly mobilize to 20,000 to 25,000. It is the only force stationed in central Baghdad and in the Republican Palace, although these are also brigades of the Special Security Service (SSO), the Iraqi Intelligence Service (IIS), and secret police in the city.

■ The 1st Brigade is headquartered at Hayy Al-Qadisiyeh in Baghdad and has five battalions, including ones stationed in the Republican palace and at Saddam International Airport. Additional battalions, including plain-clothes units, are assigned to protect Saddam while he is in transit and are assigned to guard other palaces and facilities.

■ The 2nd Brigade is headquartered at the Al Rashid military base and has combat-experience elements outside Baghdad and in the Mosul area.

■ The 3rd Brigade is headquartered at Taji and has four combat battalions to defend Taji and the approaches to Baghdad.

■ The 4th Brigade, which is motorized, is located at Al Harithiyeh and Al Quadis-iyeh, and defends the southern outskirts of Baghdad.

■ The Armor Command (4th Armored Brigade) has T-72s, BMP-1 and BMP-2s, and two armored regiments, one located at the Abu-Ghraib Camp, and another near the Al-Makasib village. They provide armored forces to defend the major entrance points to the city.

The sheer scale of the forces protecting the regime is illustrated by an estimate by Amatzia Baram, who puts the total number of men involved in the various internal security and intelligence organizations at more than 100,000, and possibly as high as 150,000, excluding the Republican Guard but including some 30,000 in the police forces and 20,000 border guards.[9] The Military Intelligence Service, or Al Estikhbarat al Askariyya, alone is a 3,000–5,000-man element with a major complex in the Aladhamia area of Baghdad. It also has a base at the Al Rashid Camp and elements in Kirkuk, Mosul, and Basra. The Special Branch is organized to carry out covert operations, infiltrate opposition movements, and provide internal security operations within the military. The Military Security Service, or al Amn al Askariyya, reports directly to the Presidential Palace and deals with subversion within the military forces.

All of these forces have significant limitations. The army and internal security forces have lost many of their personnel with combat experience; in the decade since the Gulf War, Iraqi forces have had limited exercise training and have never mastered combined arms and joint operations by Western standards. Saddam Hussein's regime has always given internal security against coups a much higher priority than military effectiveness per se. There were exceptions during the most threatening periods in the Iran-Iraq war, but many of the best officers were retired or shoved aside into positions of limited importance, and some suffered suspicious fatal accidents. Political control has not only affected independence and initiative, but has extended to the point of limiting or preventing the use of ammunition in live-fire exercises, the scale of maneuver exercises, and forward stockage of ammunition and supplies that might be used in a coup. Iraqi forces have, however, had ongoing low-level combat experience against the Shi'ite opposition in Southern Iraq and often deploy to positions opposite Iran and the Kurdish security zone. They do conduct static fire training and limited maneuver training, and the Special Republican Guard, Republican Guard, and security forces are trained for urban warfare and putting down uprisings. The Republican Guard units never broke during the Gulf War, and the army's regular armored, mechanized, and commando/special forces units have generally fought with considerable determination when ordered to do so.

Iraq has other problems. Saddam exercises tight central control in his self-appointed role as field marshall, and innovation and initiative are often discouraged. Additional problems are created by Saddam's rotation and sometimes violent purges of commanders to ensure loyalty, promotion for loyalty or because of tribal origin, ruthlessness of the security services, and tensions among regular forces, Republican Guards, Special Republican Guards, and various security services.

Although a number of seemingly convincing reports of security, problems, defections, and coup attempts have proved false, at least some seem to be correct, and it is far from clear that the situation has improved in spite of Iraq's increasing

---

9. Amatzia Baram, "The Iraqi Armed Forces and Security Apparatus," *Journal of Conflict, Security and Development,* Centre for Defense Studies (London: King's College, 2001): 113–123.

oil income and the regime's ability to manipulate oil-for-food deliveries. Professional security services cannot challenge regular armed forces and rarely succeed in suppressing large-scale popular revolts. Large unprofessional security services have limited value. Saddam has tried on several past occasions to create a parallel popular force that would act as a further check upon the regular forces. Such forces failed dismally during the Iran-Iraq War. The latest such effort is the so-called Jerusalem Army, which has been created since the start of the Second Intifada and is under General Iyad Futayyih Khalifa al-Rawi, a former Republican Guard commander. This force is reported to have a goal of 21 divisions, but Iraq lacks the experienced cadres, equipment, supplies, and manpower input to build up anything like such a force except at the cost of its other land-force units.[10]

The Iraqi Air Force

The Iraqi Air force has around 30,000 men. It still has some 316 combat aircraft, although only about 50 percent to 60 percent are serviceable. Senior pilots still fly 60 to 120 hours a year depending on the aircraft, but junior pilots fly as few as 20.

The IISS estimates that the air force has 6 obsolete H-6D and Tu-22 bombers and 130 attack aircraft. These include Mirage F-1EQs, Su-20s, 40 Su-22s, 2 Su-24s, and 2 Su-25s. Iraq still has extensive stocks of short-range air-to-ground missiles and cluster bombs. It also has 180 air defense fighters, including 12 MiG-25s, 50 Mirage F-1EQs, and 10 MiG-29s, plus 5 MiG-25 reconnaissance aircraft. Additionally, the air force has extensive stocks of MiG-21s, training aircraft, and drones, and has experimented with using them as unmanned aerial vehicles (UAVs) and unmanned combat aerial vehicles (UCAVs). It still has 2 IL-76 tankers and large numbers of transport aircraft.

Jane's provides a different estimate with the following key combat types; the number estimated to be in service are shown in parentheses: 40(0) F-7s, 30 (13) Mirage F-1EQs, 36 (15–25) Mig-21s, 35 (15–20) Mig23s, 6 (3–6) MiG-25s, 17 (1) Mig-29s, 33 (15–18) Su-20/22s, 21 (6–11) Su-25s, 2 T-22s, and 3 Tu-16s.[11]

Air force air-to-air and air-to-ground training is limited and unrealistic. In the past, command and control has been overcentralized and mission planning has often set impossible goals. The two no-fly zones have further limited air training and combat experience. There are no modern airborne sensor, command-and-control, or intelligence capabilities other than a small number of UAVs. Air control and warning still heavily depend on outdated ground-based intercept capabilities. The air force has, however, practiced penetration raids by single low-flying aircraft and has shown that it can conduct independent offensive operations at the small formation level.

The heavy surface-to-air missile forces of the Air Defense Command are still organized into one of the densest defensive networks in the world. There are four regional air defense centers at Kirkuk (north), Kut al Hayy (east), Al Basra (south),

---

10. Ibid.

11. *Jane's Sentinel Security Assessments,* "Iraqi Air Force," online edition, accessed May 7, 2002.

and Ramadia (west). Major command facilities are underground and hardened. Additionally, there is a network of redundant radars and optical fibre command links. Reports differ over the extent to which China has helped Iraq create a modern and highly survivable optical fibre command net. There are unconfirmed reports of more modern radars being smuggled in from Ukraine.

The system is backed by extensive low-altitude anti-aircraft (AA) guns and SA-8b, SA-11, and SA-13 short- and medium-range missiles. The Sterla 2 and 10 (SA-7 and SA-10) are used for terminal defense of key buildings. Iraq has learned to rapidly move its fire units and sensors and to use urban cover and decoys, "pop-on radar" guidance techniques, and optical tracking. Its mix of SA-2s, SA-3s, and SA-6s is badly outdated, but some modifications have been made.

Iraq has learned a great deal about land-based air defense operations from the Gulf War and more than 10 years of operations against the U.S. and British aircraft enforcing the no-fly zones. Iraq provided significant aid to Serbia in air defense tactics during the fighting in Kosovo and helped Serbia make effective use of decoys, "pop-on" and remotely linked radar activity, various ambush tactics, and the use of deployments in civilian areas to limit NATO's ability to strike at targets because of the possibility of collateral damage or civilian casualties.

Iraq is certain to have developed contingency plans to move and disperse its land-based air defenses in the event of a major U.S.-led attempt to overthrow the regime and to try to concentrate such defenses to protect the regime and use them partially to compensate for the lack of an effective Iraqi air force. To strike, Iraq has developed some countermeasures to U.S. anti-radiation missiles since the Gulf War and has recently begun to obtain significant equipment through Syria.

The Iraqi Navy

The 2,000-man Iraqi navy, which was never an effective force, was devastated during the Gulf War. It now has only six obsolete Osa and Bogomol guided missile patrol craft and three obsolete Soviet inshore minesweepers. Iraq does, however, retain all of the shore-based Silkworm and other anti-ship missiles it had at the time of the Gulf War and extensive stocks of mines—some of them relatively modern and sophisticated. (The United States never succeeded in targeting land-based Iraqi anti-ship missiles during the Gulf War, and the U.S. and British Navies entered Iraqi mine fields without detecting their presence.)

Iraqi Operational Capabilities

It is difficult to generalize about Iraqi forces where each land and air unit has such different levels of effectiveness and where political and internal security considerations are so important. However, Iraq has demonstrated that it can still carry out significant ground force exercises and fly relatively high sortie rates. It has not, however, demonstrated training patterns that show its army has consistent levels of training, can make effective use of combined arms above the level of some individual brigades, or has much capability for joint land-air operations. It also has not demonstrated that it can use surface-to-air missiles in a well-organized way as a maneuvering force to cover its deployed land forces.

Iraq does retain the ability to rapidly move heavy armored forces by tank transporter if it can use its road net and does not face major air opposition. Republican Guard and regular army armored and mechanized divisions probably can fight well from defensive positions, though such tactics did little to ensure their survivability in the Gulf War because of U.S. superiority in air power, attack helicopters, thermal sights, and range of engagement. Iraqi artillery outranges U.S. tube artillery, but the advantage has little or no operational meaning because Iraq has very limited targeting capability beyond visual range, has not developed the capability to rapid shift fires, and has limited artillery maneuverability. Iraq conscript forces receive comparatively limited training, reserve training is largely in-unit training or no training at all, the Iraqi NCO corps is weak, junior officers receive rote training and are given limited initiative, and combined arms and manpower management focuses on loyalty rather than effectiveness.

Iraq made poor use of fixed and rotary wing combat aircraft in close support and interdiction missions throughout the Iran-Iraq War and never had the chance to conduct such operations during the Gulf War. Contrary to Iraqi opposition reports—which seek to transfer the blame for the failure of their postwar uprisings to the United States—Iraq never needed to make extensive use of attack helicopters to suppress their uprisings. It was able to rely on its virtual monopoly of armor and artillery.

Iraq's infrastructure and combat engineering is now better than its combat forces. Iraq has been able to rebuild many of the shelters and facilities it lost during the Gulf War and much of the air force combat, command, control, communications, and intelligence/battlefield management (C^4I/BM) system. This C^4I/BM system included an extensive net of optical fiber communications net, a TFH 647 radio relay system, a TFH tropospheric communications system, and a large mix of radars supplied by the Soviet Union. Iraq has rebuilt most of the air bases damaged during the Gulf War, and a number of bases received only limited damage. This gives Iraq a network of some 25 major operating bases, many with extensive shelters and hardened facilities.[12]

Iraq retains chemical and biological weapons and is believed to have anywhere from 15–80 Scud missile assemblies of various types. But there is no way to know how lethal these weapons really are, how Iraq would deploy them, what plans it has to use them, or the regime's command and control arrangements. Most experts do not believe Iraq has nuclear weapons or any significant domestic ability to produce fissile materials. Ex-IAEA inspectors do believe, however, that Iraq retains all of the

---

12. Many different lists exist of the names of such bases. Jane's lists Al Amarah, Al Asad, Al Bakr, Al Basrah–West Maqal, Al Khalid, Al Kut, Al Qayyarah, Al Rashid, Al Taqaddum, Al Walid, Artawi, As Salman, As Samara, As Zubair, Baghdad-Muthenna, Balada, Bashur, Erbil, Jalibah, Karbala, Radif al Khafi, Kirkuk, Mosul, Mudaysis, Nejef, Qal'at Sikar, Qurna, Rumaylah, Safwan, Shibah, Shyaka Mayhar, Sulyamaniya, Tal Afar, Tallil-As Nasiryah, Tammuz, Tikrit, Ubdaydah bin al Jarrah, and Wadi Al Khirr. Many of the bases on this list are of limited size or are largely dispersal facilities. See Jane's Sentinel Security Assessments, "The Gulf States: Iraq," London, various editions.

technology needed to make moderately sized implosion weapons if it can obtain fissile material. It has developed its own initiators, HE lenses, and switching devices.

The Problem of Sanctions and Equipment Modernization

Sanctions and the impact of the Gulf War have had a major impact on Iraqi warfighting capabilities. Iraq has not been able to fund or import any major new conventional warfare technology to react to the lessons of the Gulf War, nor has it produced any major equipment—with the possible exception of limited numbers of Magic "dogfight" air-to-air missiles. Iraq's inability to recapitalize and modernize its forces means that much of its large order of battle is now obsolescent or obsolete, has uncertain combat readiness, and will be difficult to sustain in combat. It also raises serious questions about the ability of Iraq's forces to conduct long-range movements or maneuvers and then sustain coherent operations.

Iraq has, however, maintained much of the clandestine arms-purchasing network that it set up during the time of the Iran-Iraq War. It has prior experience in buying from some 500 companies in 43 countries and has set up approximately 150 small purchasing companies or agents. Intelligence experts believe that Iraq also has an extensive network of intelligence agents and middlemen involved in arms purchases. It has probably obtained some air defense equipment from countries like Ukraine and China and may have been able to smuggle in some spare parts through Syria, Turkey, and Jordan. Deliveries through Syria, which have become significant since mid-2001, include parts and weapons assemblies for MIG and Shukoi aircraft, armor, and land-based air defenses. Nevertheless, Iraq has not been able to restructure its overall force to compensate for its prior dependence on an average of $3 billion a year in arms deliveries. It has not visibly deployed any major new weapon system since 1991, nor has it been able to recapitalize any aspect of its force structure. About two-thirds of its remaining inventory of armor and aircraft are obsolete by Westerns standards. Iraq has lacked the funds, spare parts, and production capabilities to sustain the quality of its consolidated forces. Although it has domestic military production facilities, it is limited to the production of guns and ammunition and has never succeeded in mass-producing more advanced weapons. Many of its modernization efforts have shown some technical skill, but others have been little more than unintentional technical practical jokes.

In contrast, Saudi Arabia alone has taken delivery on more than $66 billion worth of new arms since 1991. Kuwait has received $7.6 billion, Iran $4.3 billion, Bahrain $700 million, Oman $1.4 billion, Qatar $1.7 billion, and the UAE $7.9 billion. Equally important, the United States has made major upgrades in virtually every aspect of its fighter avionics, attack munitions, cruise missile capabilities, and intelligence, reconnaissance, and targeting capabilities.

The Problem of Dynamic Net Assessment

Translating the foregoing evaluation of Iraqi military capabilities into some form of "dynamic net assessment" is far more difficult than making broad generalizations about the size and readiness of Iraqi military forces. A dynamic net assessment means that Iraqi capabilities have to be compared with specific threat forces in specific contingencies, a task that presents two major complications:

- First, the war-fighting capabilities of Iraqi forces are heavily affected by a wide range of uncertainties and intangibles, and traditional analyses of order of battle and of weapons types and effectiveness are more likely to mislead than inform.

- Second, there is a wide range of contingencies that can affect Iraq's future, and a dynamic assessment of one preferred contingency cannot explain either Iraq's probable capabilities or the range of uncertainties involved. In a number of such contingencies, the political impact of Iraq's military capabilities is likely to be more important than its war-fighting capability. In other contingencies, Iraq is virtually forced to engage in asymmetric warfare. In fact, Iraq has every reason to avoid the kind of "conventional" battles that could involve U.S.-led coalitions fighting on terms unfavorable to them.

Uncertainties and Intangibles

Wars and battles are rarely decided by "tangible" factors like manpower and equipment numbers, quantifiable aspects of sustainability, or other measures of effectiveness. One historical case after another shows the real-world outcome of war has been determined by "intangibles," where various experts differ sharply over the relative capability of each side. Today some experts find it very easy to assert that Iraq's major combat units will fight with loyalty and determination because of their privileges, dependence on the regime, and nationalism. Others find it equally easy to assert that Iraqi forces will rapidly collapse or defect because the regime is an unpopular tyranny.

In practice, Iraq's performance in past wars has shown that many aspects of its military behavior cannot be predicted until a war starts and that these uncertainties interact with the uncertainties affecting any predictions about the military performance of Iraq's opponents. The following "intangibles" and uncertainties regarding Iraqi war-fighting capability affect any dynamic net assessment of Iraq:

- Real-world popularity and unpopularity of the regime among the various elements of the armed forces and in areas of military operations; loyalty that may vary across different force elements, such as Republican Guards, Special Republican Guards, regular army with regular manning, and regular army with largely conscript manning

- Real-world impact of repression and tyranny versus incentives, nationalism, and propaganda in determining popular support for the regime or active opposition; the impact of issues like ethnic divisions, UN sanctions and the oil for food program, and backlash from the Second Intifada

- Willingness of various Kurdish factions to participate in, or ride out, a conflict

- Loyalty of various Shi'ite elements to Saddam Hussein's regime versus willingness to join in uprisings and active resistance

- Efficacy of the regime's bribes and incentives in buying loyalty

- Impact by combat element of more than 10 years without open access to world arms market, along with limited discretionary funding for force maintenance and modernization; and limitation on ability past ability to smuggle in parts, weapons, and munitions

- Uncertain sustainability of current stock of munitions and spare parts

- Quality of training and leadership experience by unit and force element

- Reliance on a rigid logistic system, emphasizing "flood forward" techniques to make up for a lack of response to the needs of commanders and the tactical situation, by moving supplies forward in large amounts, regardless of the immediate need

- Progress in reducing the past rigidities and overcentralization of the command system and its failure to allow for independence of action

- Real-world ability to execute urban warfare and military operations in built-up areas; also, the ability to shelter in populated areas, and use human shields, without popular uprisings or action. Impact of ethnic divisions, tribal loyalties, etc., in given areas

- Level of improvement in air operations and in ability to conduct effective air-to-air and air-to-ground combat using dispersed forces capable of independent operations

- Efficiency of dispersal techniques and human shields, plus decoys and deception, in limiting the efficacy of U.S. intelligence and strategic reconnaissance (ISR), targeting, and air strike capabilities

- Ability to make effective use of water barriers and earth barriers; ability to tie combat engineering to real-world military tactics in the face of U.S. airpower and helicopter mobility

- Ability to effectively deploy and concentrate air defense assets for tactical purposes, versus exploit largely fixed SA-2/ SA-3 and SA-6 system

■ Short- and medium-term wartime survivability of heavy surface-to-air missile defenses

■ Current status of joint warfare and combined arms expertise and improvement in such expertise, if any

■ Cohesive maneuvering capability and ability to use helicopters to overcome water barriers and to reinforce

■ Since 1991, improvements in artillery tactics and methods to acquire long-range targeting capabilities and manage and switch fires

■ Planning and real-world capability to execute asymmetric and covert warfare and use terrorist proxies

■ Effectiveness of the security and paramilitary forces in the face of any serious popular opposition

■ Size and effectiveness of Iraqi opposition forces, if any

■ Size and effectiveness of current holdings of chemical, biological, radiological, and nuclear (CBRN) weapons and missiles and other delivery systems; possible possession of a biological or nuclear weapon so lethal that it could inflict massive damage or casualties and make a major change in the level of deterrence or war-fighting capability

■ Existence of preplanned launch on warning (LOW), launch under attack (LUA), and retaliatory strike capability to deliver CBRN forces; deployment of covert and terrorist proxy capabilities.

It is easy to guess at—or to assert—some judgment about Iraqi capability in any of the above areas. It is certainly true that little about Iraqi military behavior since 1991 implies that Iraq will suddenly achieve dramatic degrees of surprise and innovation in military operations; however, this can scarcely be ruled out, and the key issue in war fighting is often one of marginal or relative efficiency.

In a contingency, like a U.S.-led invasion to overthrow Saddam, Iraq *may* have enough war-fighting capability to require a very significant U.S. and allied response. In many other contingencies, the weaknesses in Iraqi forces may not be critical relative to similar or different weaknesses in Iranian and other Gulf forces.

Defining the Key Contingencies

Another set of uncertainties arises because it is not possible to narrow down the range of contingencies used in any dynamic net assessment of Iraq to a few simple cases. Some U.S. planners may wish to see the issue only in terms of a U.S. effort to overthrow the Iraqi regime, but the following contingencies have enough credibility to at least merit summary discussion.

■ Iraq faces continued containment without effective inspection. The battle is one of sanctions, propaganda, and perceptions.

- Iraq faces continued containment with effective inspection. The battle is still one of sanctions, propaganda, and perceptions, but selective military action may be needed to deal with proliferation.

- The continuing low-level air war over the no-fly zones accelerates—perhaps with the downing of a U.S. or British aircraft—and the United States and UK respond.

- Iraq becomes more confident over time and feels that it can exploit the backlash against the United States from the Second Intifada and war on terrorism to make another grab for Kuwait.

- Unforeseen events thrust Iraq into another confrontation with the Kurds in the north or Shi'ites in the south.

- Unforeseen events thrust Iraq into another major war with Iran.

- Iraq takes risks in a desperate attack on Kuwait.

- Iraq threatens or begins to execute missile and air attacks using CBRN weapons or threatens an LOW/LUA response.

- "Existential response": The United States, its Gulf allies, Turkey, and/or Israel face a "broken back" Iraqi effort to strike at population centers and other key targets in retaliation for its defeat and the pending overthrow of Saddam's regime.

- Iraq carries out major attacks against the United States, Britain, Israel, or a Gulf state using covert action or a terrorist/extremist proxy.

- The United States leads a coalition in a major military effort to remove Saddam Hussein's regime and conduct "nation building" to change the basic character of the Iraqi state.

It is important to note that Iraqi war-fighting capabilities in all of the contingencies on this list are timeline dependent. Both the characterization of the contingencies and the way in which they are likely to be fought will change strikingly if Iraq can break out of sanctions and rearm; if Iraq can build up a truly sophisticated and lethal capability to deliver CBRN weapons; if U.S. operational capabilities in the Gulf should become limited for political or basing reasons; or if other strategic changes should take place in the major nations around Iraq.

Furthermore, only the most drastic contingencies involve a major change in the Iraqi regime and Iraq's future behavior. Most of the contingencies would be preludes to further struggles or confrontations. In the case of those contingencies that do involve regime change, it is far from clear that the next Iraqi regime would live peacefully in a peaceful Gulf located in a peaceful Middle East. As Haiti and other cases have shown, it is far easier to have good intentions than it is to execute them or avoid the law of unintended consequences. Even a prolonged post-Saddam nation-building effort might still result in leaving a troubled Iraq in a troubled region.

Iraq Faces Continued Containment and Air War

Iraq fully understands that diplomacy and politics are an extension of war by other means and that such a battle is one of sanctions, propaganda, and perceptions. At this point in time, Iraq is losing, to the extent that it cannot legally import arms or military equipment and cannot import dual-use items or equipment for its missile and CBRN programs.

Containment without Effective Inspection

Iraq is severely restricted by the U.S.-British air operations in the northern and southern "no-fly" zones and further constrained by the fact that the Kurds have de facto autonomy in their security zone. The United States and Britain now spend roughly $1 billion a year to enforce the two no-fly zones at a cost of some $519.5 million from January to May 2002 for the Southern Watch and $118 million for the Northern Watch. The United States and Britain have flown these patrols, though U.S. and British aircraft have been under sporadic attack ever since Operation Desert Fox. Iraq seriously threatened U.S. and British aircraft on 143 occasions in 1999, 145 in 2000, 97 in 2001, and 32 as of June 2002. The United States and Britain returned fire 102 times in 1999, 48 in 2002, 11 in 2001, and 22 times since the beginning of this fiscal year in October 2001—14 times in executing Southern Watch and 8 in executing Northern Watch.[13]

The combination of an inability to carry out large-scale and well-organized conventional arms imports and the constant presence of U.S. and British airpower has a powerful effect. It severely limits Iraqi modernization while the bulk of Iraqi forces deteriorate. At the same time, Iraq faces major limits on any ability to train for joint warfare and deploy its forces—although the severe constraints on its conventional capabilities do act as another major incentive to proliferate. Iraq also faces the problem that if it ever is successful in shooting down a U.S. or British aircraft—what some of those enforcing the no-fly zones call a "magic bullet"—the United States and Britain have a virtual invitation to massively retaliate against critical Iraqi leadership, military, and CBRN facilities. Iraq might score a limited propaganda "triumph," but suffer far more than it did during Desert Fox.

Saddam Hussein's regime also faces major restrictions on its ability to use most of its oil export income as a result of UN sanctions and the oil for food program.

---

13. *Washington Post*, July 26, 2002, p. A23.

The United States and Britain have succeeded in winning broad UN support for an extended "smart sanctions" program and the renewal of UN inspection under the United Nations Monitoring, Verification, and Inspection Commission (UNMOVIC). In spite of a growing volume of smuggling, this inability to modernize and obtain munitions and spare parts openly and efficiently ensures the steady deterioration of Iraq's conventional forces and places severe limits on its missile developments, which must at least appear to involve systems with ranges of 150 kilometers or less. Additional restrictions force Iraq to keep its CBRN developments covert.

On the other hand, Iraq is winning to the extent that it has now been free of any meaningful UN weapons inspections for four years, has avoided full inspection since early 1997, and can carry out missile development while claiming to comply with the 150-kilometer limit on its missiles. Iraq again refused any meaningful UN inspection effort in July 2002. It blamed the United States and Britain for the breakdown and accused the Bush administration of being responsible for the lack of progress on the grounds that they only wanted inspections to resume in order to help their targeting efforts in an invasion of Iraq.[14]

Iraq has substantial illegal purchasing networks overseas and has succeeded in importing significant amounts of technology for missiles and CBRN weapons, along with some parts and equipment for its conventional forces. These include substantial improvements in its C^{4}I systems, particularly in terms of optical fiber systems for its surface-to-air missile developments. Although sanctions severely limit Iraq's overt testing of missiles, its imports of large amount of chemical weapons feedstocks, and its ability to create large, visible plants to produce fissile material, they place few limits on any other aspects of Iraq's weapons of mass destruction (WMD) programs. In fact, the inability to import large conventional military equipment and the ability to carry on with covert CBRN programs act as a further incentive for Iraq to concentrate on proliferation.

Iraq also has been largely victorious in the battle of perceptions in the region, exploiting the suffering of its own people and blaming the UN and United States for the consequences of failure to comply with the terms of the cease-fire. It is skillfully exploiting the Second Intifada with such measures as paying $25,000 to the families of Palestinian suicide bombers; its diplomacy has been successful enough to persuade Turkey and all of the Arab states that they are better off living with Saddam than backing any U.S. effort to overthrow his regime.

For more than a decade, the U.S. State Department's effort to publicize Saddam's attempts to retain CBRN weapons, exploit sanctions and the oil for food program, and misuse Iraq's revenues has ranged from dismal failure to total incompetence. The United States has been equally ineffective in its systematic and continuing efforts to rebut charges that it is responsible for large numbers of Iraqi deaths resulting from the sanctions and for serious casualties and collateral damage resulting from militarily enforcing the no-fly zones. (Iraq claimed as of June 2002 that the United States and Britain had killed 1,483 Iraqis and wounded 1,400 in enforcing the no-fly zones.)[15]

---

14. *New York Times*, July 5, 2002, p. A6, and July 7, 2002, p. A4.

U.S. support of Iraqi opposition groups has so far done little more than contribute to exile politics and has had no detectable impact on Iraq. Furthermore, the United States has not succeeded in conducting a meaningful public diplomacy effort to justify its military presence in the Gulf or the value of its arms sales and military assistance efforts in the region. The United States has achieved the exact opposite of information dominance. It has created an information vacuum that Iraq has been able to exploit.

The Kurds fear any open support of a U.S. effort to overthrow Saddam. With little historical reason to trust the United States, they benefit from the status quo and from smuggling out oil and product and smuggling in forbidden items. The Shi'ite opposition is almost totally defeated, except for the occasional low-level bombing and assassination. The outside Iraqi opposition is weak, has no meaningful military capability, and is heavily penetrated by Iraqi intelligence.

Money is fungible, and Saddam has been able to use revenues from the oil for food program to help buy support for his regime. At the same time, he has directed the substantial funds he obtains from illegal exports of oil and product to fund both his military forces and his smuggling efforts in support of his conventional forces and missile and CBRN programs. Although significant political opposition remains, Saddam has been able to restore many of the incentives and payments he uses to win support for his regime. In addition, he has effectively used his propaganda war to exploit Iraqi nationalism. "Smart sanctions" have failed to do anything to halt smuggling across the Syrian, Turkish, and Jordanian borders, and UN import controls and inspection across these borders is steadily less effective.

Containment with "Effective" Inspection

Although Saddam Hussein may find many aspects of his current strategic situation to be frustrating, he may well feel that he is winning the "war of sanctions" and that time is on his side. Two major exceptions to such a conclusion are the continued threat of direct U.S. military intervention to overthrow his regime and a much broader range of outside pressures to restore UN inspections under UNMOVIC.

The Iraqi regime clearly prefers to avoid inspection. In fact, the continued threat of such inspection may sharply constrain Iraq's ability to carry out the more visible and detectable aspects of missile and CBRN development. It also requires Iraq to maintain highly dispersed, highly mobile, and duplicative programs organized into cell-like structures. Iraq has never been efficient in managing any large, complex program, and the constraints on its program almost certainly add serious problems in many areas.

If Iraq is forced to accept inspections by UNMOVIC as a consequence of threatened U.S. military action or as a result of other political factors, it will do everything possible to keep such an effort from being effective and will use it as a political weapon to obtain UN certification that it no longer is proliferating. It will systematically lie, cheat, posture, and resist, just as it did with UNSCOM. It will also put

---

15. *Washington Post*, July 26, 2002, p. A23.

intense diplomatic pressure on the UN and friendly states to avoid intrusive inspections, attempt to limit their scope, and encourage a rush to some kind of judgment, freeing itself of effective further inspections. It will draw on more than a decade of expertise in cheating inspection while most inspectors will be new and many will have to consider their nation's reservations about aggressively pursuing inspections.

Much will depend on the courage, skill, and determination of the inspectors and their leadership. The challenge of conducting effective inspections will be vastly complicated by the fact that Iraq has had four uninterrupted years not only to destroy the chain of evidence going back to its efforts before and during the Gulf War, but also to create new programs with no trace to past programs in terms of location and personnel. These problems will be compounded by additional challenges. The UNSCOM effort, which was never voluntary, only worked through constant challenge and coercion; because UNSCOM reported directly to the Security Council, it could not be paralyzed by the political inertia and divisions of the regular UN bureaucracy. UNSCOM could operate without prior warning or any Iraqi agreement as to what to inspect, what technology could be inspected, and what intelligence could be used. It had its own helicopter support and vehicles, and its movements were backed by the constant and credible threat of force.

UNSCOM also could draw freely on national intelligence, particularly from the United States and Europe. This allowed inspection to operate in the context of national intelligence on exports and arms transfers, indirect access to U.S. national technical means (NTM) and signals intelligence, and data on specific inspection targets—including NTM and U-2 imagery on mobile Iraqi activity. National sources could provide data on weapons technology unavailable to UN inspectors and provide intelligence feedback on how well the inspection effort was proceeding.

The UN may find it difficult, if not impossible, to trace most Iraqi activity. Iraq has had a decade to learn how to counter technical intelligence, control the risk of defectors, make key equipment and technology mobile, and disperse its efforts in an emergency. The UN is certain to find that Iraq has created a sophisticated set of decoys, false trails, and false compliance efforts. At the same time, Iraq cannot be sure what various intelligence agencies know or whether it will have new problems with defectors. It is all too possible that the end result of inspections could be a new set of armed clashes and a repetition of all of the frustrations of the previous International Atomic Energy Agency (IAEA)/UNSCOM effort. The worst case would be a weak effort by the UNMOVIC and a politically motivated certification that Iraq had complied with the terms of the cease-fire. In short, resuming inspection does not mean such inspection will be effective, and the "war of sanctions" will go on with or without UN inspection. More also is involved than the detection of Iraqi missile and CBRN production and deployment efforts. Saddam Hussein's Iraq has a long history of being able to go further and prepare for significant military action without the international community having or heeding strategic warning. Its preparations to attack Iran achieved considerable surprise. Its use of chemical weapons came as a surprise as did its success in deployed extended-range Scuds. IAEA inspection served little purpose before the Gulf War, and the Gulf War achieved strategic surprise in spite of the fact Iraqi preparations were detected weeks in advance. During the Gulf War, Iraq achieved some degree of surprise in terms of its attack on Khafji, the scale of its missile attacks, and burning of the Kuwaiti oil fields in spite of a massive coalition surveillance and intelligence effort.

Continuing Low-Level Air War over the No-Fly Zones

Saddam Hussein has long demonstrated that Iraq will continue to resist the U.S.-UK enforcement of the two no-fly zones and that Iraq is seeking a victory by downing a U.S. or British aircraft. The U.S.-UK enforcement of the two no-fly zones is a key factor in maintaining the containment of Iraq and the UN's ability to enforce sanctions. Iraq can be expected to oppose it by every possible military and political means. Saddam would see the ability to prevent or limit the enforcement of either or both no-fly zones as a major victory and one that sharply undermined the credibility of containment and U.S. threats to overthrow his regime.

Iraq is severely constrained in what it can do militarily, because of its inability to import new major air defense weapons and sensors and its inability to obtain overt support in modernizing its C^4I/BM program. It also cannot attend to risk the key air defense assets it needs to conserve in the event of a major U.S. attack. It has, however, developed a steadily better ability to use multiple radars and pop-up tactics to reduce the effectiveness of U.S.-UK countermeasures; has learned to limit the effectiveness of anti-radiation missiles; has developed visible tracking systems; has improved its use of decoys and dispersal; has improved its use of urban cover and human shields; and has turned exaggerated claims about civilian casualties and collateral damage into a fine art.

Iraq will claim any U.S. or British aircraft loss over Iraq as a major victory, and it will be seen as one in the region almost regardless of the U.S.-UK military response. Iraq also has sufficient air defense assets so that it appears to "win" every time another clash occurs, simply because of its ability to ride out the U.S.-UK military response and exploit new claims of collateral damage and civilian casualties.

Large-scale and effective U.S.-UK strikes in response to any Iraqi success could turn such an event into a different story, but have to be carefully structured so they have a clear provocation, produce serious damage to Iraq's military forces and regime, and minimize collateral damage and civilian casualties. Even the major strikes that took place during Desert Fox were a failure in this regard, because they were not targeted well enough and sustained long enough to do serious damage, and the "pinprick" response now taking place has little or no deterrent effect.

Iraq Becomes More Confident over Time

The "timelines" and forces shaping Iraq's current strategic position remain unclear. Iraq is not necessarily winning. It will, however, continue to covertly develop its missile and CBRN programs to the maximum extent it feels it can get away with and will continue to rebuild its conventional strength to the extent it can smuggle in arms, spare parts, and munitions—or can eventually ease sanctions.

Iraq may or may not be able to restore its military strength and strategic position to the point where it can actively play the role of a revanchist state. A reinvasion of Kuwait seems less probable, although a ruthless suppression of the Kurdish security zone seems a near certainty, at some point in the future if Iraq remains under Saddam Hussein.

Iraqi revanchist actions, through covert operations and the support of terrorist or extremist groups, seem all too possible. A systematic exploitation of the tensions and backlash from the Second Intifada is already under way.

Similarly, Iraq is likely to engage in "wars of intimidation" and eventually to use its growing CBRN capabilities to put pressure on the southern Gulf states over oil policy and quotas and their willingness to support the U.S. and British military presence and power projection capabilities. A militarily "confident" Saddam Hussein is also likely to pressure Turkey to end its support for the northern no-fly zone, ease its enforcement of the UN sanctions, and play a far more active role in trying to win Arab support through support of the Second Intifada. The resulting Iraqi-Syrian-Palestinian, and possible Jordanian, cooperation could pose a growing security threat to the region.

CHAPTER 4

Iraq versus Its Neighbors

Unforeseen Events Thrust Iraq into Another Confrontation with the Kurds or Shi'ites

Iraq could win any future conflict with its Kurdish population in the north or its Shi'ite population in the south, and Saddam Hussein's regime would take major risks to do so if it believed any serious attempt was being made to use them as a sanctuary for building up meaningful opposition in military capabilities or staging facilities for a U.S. presence that was not part of a major U.S. military effort to secure the area involved.

Kurdish Contingencies

At this point in time, Iraq has little incentive to conduct military operations against the Kurdish security zone. It is certain to produce a major new wave of U.S. air attacks and might well trigger a U.S.-led invasion to overthrow Saddam. The Kurds remain divided and comparatively isolated. Consequently, they act as a buffer against any serious Turkish ambitions in Iraq; however, Iraq can count on Turkey to intervene if they do develop a more effective military threat. Their "sanctuary" status helps Iraq maintain the flow of uncontrolled oil and product sales, and Iraq may well calculate that it can ride out international interest in the Kurds and forcibly reintegrate them back into Iraq in the future.

The Kurds, in turn, have only limited reason to try to fight Iraq unless they can be absolutely sure of both victory and the political aftermath. They have good reason to feel that the West has betrayed them in the past. They no have more autonomy than at any other time in their recent history, and U.S. and British aircraft help give them security by patrolling the northern no-fly zone.

The Kurds have made real progress in creating a modern enclave in the zone, funded in part by oil for food money and in part by smuggling.[16] They are, however, still divided between two major factions led by quasi-warlords. The first faction, which dominates the northwest, is the Kurdistan Democratic Party (KDP) led by Massoud Barzani and headquartered in Erbil. The second, which dominates the southeast, is the Patriotic Union of Kurdistan (PUK) led by Jalal Talibani and headquartered in Sulaimaniya. Some Turkish Kurds still operate in the area as do some Islamist and tribal factions.

On paper, the KDP claims a strength of 15,000, plus 25,000 tribesmen, armed with mortars, automatic weapons, artillery, multiple rocket launchers (MRLs), and

---

16. For a good discussion of these issues, see John F. Burns, "Kurds, Secure in North Iraq, Are Cool to a US Offensive," *New York Times*, July 8, 2002, pp. A-1 and A-7.

some SA-7s. The PUK claims strength of 10,000, plus 22,000 tribesmen, armed with automatic weapons, mortars, some artillery, AA guns, and some SA-7s. The Socialist Party of Kurdistan claims several hundred fighters.[17] There are also armed elements of the Jund al-Islam, a Kurdish Islamist extremist movement affiliated with Al Qaeda that has been involved in clashes with the PUK.[18]

Cosmetic efforts have been made to integrate some KDP and PUK forces into an integrated force, but these efforts have made limited progress. Although the Kurds can be effective mountain fighters in small, defensive engagements, they so far have only developed symbolic military capabilities. Worse, the KDP and PUK have demonstrated in the past that their paramilitary forces are not particularly competent even in fighting each other. It would take years and major reequipment to give Kurdish forces serious military capabilities.

Now and indefinitely into the future, Iraqi military forces could rapidly reenter the Kurdish security zone and defeat the Kurdish factions in settled areas in a matter of days. Kurdish guerrillas might survive in some mountainous areas or as dispersed units hiding in populated areas, but Iraq's ability to use helicopter mobility and airpower, plus long-range artillery, should be as decisive over time as it has been in the past. The main barrier to such an operation is the risk that the United States will intervene decisively with airpower, and there are limits to the deterrent value of this risk. Iraq can probably provoke further intra-Kurdish fighting as an excuse or find some faction to invite it to intervene.

The Iraqi leadership would probably be willing to absorb serious damage and losses from the air if they felt that the Kurdish leaders were willing to see the Kurdish area used as an enclave for building up armed opposition forces, or to prevent any U.S. staging in the security zone. If this seemed possible, Turkey and the Arab world would probably not support U.S. military action if the provocation was any unilateral formal Kurdish declaration of autonomy and would oppose such action if the Kurds declared independence. Kurdish civilians can be used as shelter or hostages or to put massive refugee pressure on Turkey.

Shi'ite Contingencies

Saddam Hussein's regime has already won the battle against the Shi'ites in the south and has largely eliminated the marsh areas as a sanctuary. Iraqi security forces have been strengthened in virtually every area where hostile Shi'ite elements have operated, and a decade of systematic arrests and purges, mixed with bribes and cooption, have further weakened Shi'ite resistance. The romanticized picture of the previous Shi'ite uprisings disguises the fact that they were smaller than generally reported, that helicopters were not needed to suppress them, and that some Shi'ite security forces and military turned against the uprisings in the south when they took on a religious character and when the Iranian-backed opposition became involved.

Iranian-backed guerrillas in the forces of the Supreme Council for Islamic Resistance in Iraq (SCIRI)—or Supreme Assembly of the Islamic Revolution in Iraq

---

17. These estimates are based upon the IISS, *Military Balance, 2001–2002*.
18. *Washington Times*, July 10, 2002, p. 15.

(SAIRI)—have regular combat forces based in Iran. This force is variously esti-mated at 4,000–10,000 men and has artillery and armor, although it was cut to pieces in a matter of minutes when it encountered regular Iraqi forces during the Iran-Iraq War. The Ayatollah Mohammed Bakr Hakim who leads SARI is based in Tehran, and SAIRI's forces have an extensive intelligence service and also carry out guerilla operations in Iraq. They can still carry out small operations sporadically, and there is still serious Shi'ite political opposition to the regime in some areas.

Although SAIRI is Iranian-backed and does not support any U.S. ground inter-vention in Iraq, it has approached the United States informally for air support. At least some Iranian officials also seem to be more open to Iranian-SAIRI alliances with other opposition groups and powers—although the Iranian government still officially opposes any form of U.S. military intervention and Iranian hard-liners are worried that the United States might see its concern about the "axis of evil" as a reason to use intervention in Iraq to "encircle" Iran and as the first step in a similar intervention in Iran.[19]

Many of the other leaders and defectors in the Iraq opposition movements based in the West are also Shi'ite, but the claims of such movements to have actually carried out attacks and sabotage in the south often seem grossly exaggerated or spurious.

Even SAIRI's capabilities seem to be declining. Iraqi security forces not only dominate Shi'ite areas, they also can operate with near total freedom of operation. The United States has never tried to use airpower to protect the Shi'ites in the south, and Iraqi security forces are now so embedded in Shi'ite towns and areas that it is doubtful that anything other than a massive air war with major strikes in towns and populated areas could begin to be effective in "liberating" Shi'ite areas.

Reaction to a U.S.-led Coalition

This situation would probably be very different, however, if the United States dem-onstrated that a U.S.-led coalition capable of decisively defeating Iraqi ground and security forces was going to be deployed and that U.S.-led ground forces were pre-pared to occupy the country. Under these conditions, Iraqi main force units would be tied up in combat with the U.S.-led coalition forces, the Kurds might rush to join the coalition to establish political influence after the cease-fire, and Shi'ite uprisings might well take place in areas where the security forces were believed to be weak or isolated. Various Shi'ite factions might compete to try to control populated areas, and Iranian-backed Shi'ite forces might infiltrate into Iraq or try to carry out more conventional military operations in another effort to establish credibility and influ-ence after the defeat of the Saddam Hussein regime. (SCIRI forces claim to have some 4,000 troops in Iran equipped as a light mechanized brigade equivalent. In practice, they amount to a reinforced battalion equivalent at most.)

One key point: Neither the Kurds nor the Shi'ites seem likely to respond to such an attack by deliberately dividing Iraq. Iraqi Kurds would face a future with a largely hostile Turkey and Iraq on their borders and little effective international support and sympathy. They have much more to gain from autonomy and influence than

---

19. Interviews in the region in 2000 and 2001, and *Los Angeles Times*, July 16, 2002, p. 1.

becoming a vulnerable mini-state. There might be some infighting, but not major civil war.

Similarly, most Iraqi Shi'ites are Arabs and nationalists, not separatists. Many have fought Iran in the past, and most probably have little interest in being tied to Iranian-backed movements. They too may struggle for influence and power within a post-Saddam Iraq, and there could be serious infighting. This, however, is very different from seeking to be part of a separate country.

If there is a risk, it would lie more in a U.S. failure to focus on conducting a large enough operation to maintain stability throughout Iraq, along with a failure to develop an effective coalition effort for post-conflict nation building. As Afghanistan has shown, the fact that the Bush administration may be embarrassed by the term "nation building" represents an intellectual failure on the part of some of its senior officials that they need to acknowledge and then correct. Similarly, those U.S. military officers who cannot see that conflict termination and post-conflict reconstruction are a vital part of any grand strategy are simply incompetent individuals that should resign or be removed from command. Whether or not the Bush administration likes the term, it needs to accept the mood for the activity.

Iraq versus Iran

Neither Iran nor Iraq is in a good position to resume a major war. Iran lost 40 percent to 60 percent of its major land force equipment during the climactic battles of the Iran-Iraq War in 1988. Iran has, however, rebuilt many of the military capabilities it lost during its defeat by Iraq and now has a comparatively large number of forces. Iran currently has armed forces consisting of some 513,000 men, plus 200,000 low-graded reserves. It has an army with 4 corps, 4 armored divisions, 6 infantry divisions, 2 commando and special forces divisions, and 16–20 small Iranian Revolutionary Guard Corps (IRGC) units. Like Iraq, Iran deploys substantial portions of its land forces near the Iran-Iraq border and sees operations in the border area as a major priority.

The Iranian army and IRGC have a total of around 450,000 men—including roughly 125,000 Revolutionary Guards and an inventory of some 1,135 main battle tanks, 1,200 other armored vehicles, and 1,950 towed, 290 self-propelled, and 665+ MRL major artillery weapons. The army has large numbers of mortars, 1,700 AA guns, and AT-3, AT-5, and TOW anti-tank guided weapons. It has unmanned aerial vehicles (UAVs), 100 AH-1J attack helicopters, and more than 400 utility and lift helicopters; the readiness of these aircraft, however, is low.[20]

Iran's 45,000-man air force has more than 280 combat aircraft with potential operational status. It has about 150 aging and worn U.S. fighters, which include 66 F-4D/E and 25 F-14A/B that are about 60 percent serviceable. It has 24 Su-24 and 30 MiG-29 Soviet-made fighters and Chinese F-7Ms. These are believed to be about

---

20.   These Iranian force estimates are based largely upon Anthony H. Cordesman, *Iran's Military Forces in Transition* (Westport: Praeger, 1999); IISS, *Military Balance, 2001–2002*, and material in the Internet edition of *Jane's Sentinel Security Assessments* series, accessed in June 2002.

80 percent serviceable. It has 14 RF-4E reconnaissance aircraft and 5 P-3F and 5 C-130H-MR maritime reconnaissance aircraft. It has significant transport aircraft and limited tanker capability. Its land-based surface-to-air missile defenses are an awkward blend of U.S.-made sensors and 100 IHawk missile launchers and Russian/Chinese-made sensors, and 10 SA-5, 45 HQ-21, 30 Rapier, 15 Tigercat, and an unknown number of FM-80 missile launchers.

Unlike Iraq, Iran has significant naval forces, with 18,000 regulars and 20,000 naval guards. Over the last decade, it has made major improvements in its ability to threaten maritime traffic through the Gulf and its ability to conduct unconventional warfare. It has 5 submarines, 3 aging missile frigates, and 2 aging corvettes. Additionally, it has 10 Kaman missile patrol boats and 10 Houdong missile patrol boats, most of which are equipped with C-802 anti-ship missiles. Other Iranian naval assets include two minelayers and five mine countermeasure vessels, as well as large stocks of mines. It has anti-submarine warfare (ASW) and mine warfare helicopters, and large stocks of land-based anti-ship missiles, including Silkworms. Further, the Iranian air force can deliver C-801 anti-ship missiles.

Iran is seeking to acquire modern Soviet combat aircraft and modern surface-to-air missiles, like the Russian S-300 series. It has 120 export versions of the T-72 and 440 BMPs and is seeking to import or produce more modern armor. Iran has not, however, been able to offset the obsolescence and wear of its overall inventory of armor, ships, and aircraft. Additionally, it has not been able to modernize key aspects of its military capabilities, such as airborne sensors and C^4I/BM, electronic warfare, land-based air defense integration, beyond-visual-range air-to-air combat, night warfare capabilities, stand-off attack capability, armored sensors and fire control systems, artillery mobility and battle management, combat ship systems integration, etc.

Iran has significant numbers of Scud missiles, extended-range North Korean Scuds, and Chinese CSS-8 missiles, and is developing a longer-range Shehab 3 missile. It has extensive stocks of chemical weapons, including mustard and nerve gas and possibly blood agents. Although it has bought extensive equipment for biological warfare, its capabilities remain unclear. Iran has had a nuclear weapons program since the time of the Shah, but does not seem to have any active enrichment capabilities. It can probably design efficient implosion weapons and produce every component except for the fissile material.

The end result is a mix of forces that closely approximates those of Iraq. Today neither nation has a decisive edge over the other or seems likely to acquire such an edge without major new arms imports or some substantial breakthrough in CBRN warfare capability. As a result, any new conflict between Iran and Iraq is likely to be a bloody stalemate in the border area, similar to the Iran-Iraq War. Neither side seems likely to risk such a war without political provocation of a kind that currently does not exist.

One case that might change this situation would be some kind of major uprising in Iraq's Shi'ite areas following a coup or the fall of Saddam Hussein. If Iraq suddenly seemed vulnerable, if its army seemed unable to resist, and if no strong U.S.-led force existed to deter such adventures, Iran might risk intervening in support of Iraq's Shi'ites. A power vacuum or very weak regime in Iraq might also act as an incentive for Iranian military action.

Iran, however, is too weak to challenge the United States or a U.S.-led coalition in the air and would be highly vulnerable to U.S. air and missile attacks. It also would experience substantial problems with projecting ground forces deep into Iraq and giving them suitable support and sustainment. As a result, Iran might protest major U.S.-led military intervention in Iraq but is unlikely to take the risk of using major military forces to either prevent such intervention or try to seize some share of Iraq. Iran may be a strong military power by Gulf standards, but it is a weak one by global standards and those of the United States.

As for timeliness, the Iranian-Iraqi military balance appears quite stable in the short to near term, and there is no sign that either state will achieve a decisive edge over the other in the near to mid term. The fear that as a result of continued sanctions Iraq will become relatively weaker than Iran has no military merit, and Iran is not strong enough to exploit Iraq's weakness in any contingency where a U.S.-led coalition maintains a major military presence inside Iraq.

Iraq Risks a Desperate Attack on Kuwait

It seems unlikely that Iraq would risk any further attack on Kuwait and the Southern Gulf as long as the United States maintains a major military presence in the region; indeed, the Iraqi military threat to Kuwait and Saudi Arabia should not be exaggerated. Nevertheless, Iraq does have some near-term contingency capabilities that might allow it to exploit the limits of Saudi defenses in spite of U.S. capabilities. Iraq's land forces still retain significant war-fighting capabilities and much of the force structure that made Iraq the dominant military power in the Gulf after its victory over Iran. Iraqi forces can still seize Kuwait in a matter of days or occupy part of Saudi Arabia's Eastern Province, *if* they do not face immediate opposition from U.S., Kuwaiti, and Saudi forces.

Iraq has five regular divisions located in the southern border region north of Kuwait, three of which are relatively combat-ready. There are also two Republican Guard divisions that could be rapidly deployed to support the three more capable regular divisions in an attack on Kuwait, a scenario that USCENTCOM has labeled the "Basra breakout."[21]

USCENTCOM and U.S. experts indicate that Iraq could assemble and deploy 5 heavy divisions south into Kuwait in a matter of days. It has a total of 5 Republican Guard divisions within 140 kilometers of Kuwait. Iraqi divisions now have an authorized strength of about 10,000 men. About half of the Iraqi army's 23 divisions had manning levels of around 8,000 men and "a fair state of readiness." Republican Guard divisions have an average of around 8,000 to 10,000 men. Brigades average around 2,500 men—the size of a large U.S. battalion.

Iraq would encounter major problems in assembling and deploying these forces into any kind of cohesive offensive, but Kuwait would be a potential area of weak-

---

21. USCENTCOM briefing by "senior military official."

ness in any defense of the Saudi border area by a Saudi U.S.-led coalition. The Saudi-Iraqi border area does not have any major cities or oil facilities, and Iraq would have to invade deep into the desert to reach any major Saudi target. An Iraqi seizure of Kuwait, however, would put Iraqi forces on the Saudi border at a point much nearer Saudi Arabia's critical oil facilities and population centers and astride major roads into Saudi Arabia.

USCENTCOM indicates that Kuwait could deploy only four relatively small brigades to defend its territory, two of which would be significantly less ready than the others, and Saudi Arabia would take days to deploy even one heavy brigade into areas north of Kuwait City. The tyranny of geography, Kuwait's small size, and Saudi Arabia's widely dispersed army would give Iraq an advantage in land combat in any sudden or surprise attack. The failure of Kuwait and Saudi Arabia to make more than limited cooperative defense efforts compounds the problem, as does Saudi Arabia's poor performance in modernizing its land forces and giving its air force offensive capability.

Kuwait dreamed of a 12-brigade force after the Gulf War, but it only has two combat-ready active brigades and two brigades that are more reserve units than fully active. Its land forces total only 11,000 personnel, and this total includes 1,600 foreign contract personnel, most of whom are noncombatants. The total manpower of the Kuwaiti armed forces, including the air force and navy, equals about one U.S. brigade "slice" (combat manpower plus support). The Kuwaiti army has an active tank strength of only about 75 M-84s (Yugoslav T-72s) and 174 M-1A2s. Kuwait does have active Patriot surface-to-air missile units, however, and an air force with 82 combat aircraft, including 32 F/A-18Cs and 8 F/A-18Ds.

Saudi Arabia also has important weaknesses. The Saudi army has reverted to a static defensive force that has limited effectiveness above the company and battalion level. Although it claims to have 70,000 full-time regulars in the army, plus 57,000 active members of the National Guard, actual manning levels are significantly lower. Some of its M-1A2 tanks are still in storage, plus about 145 of its 295 obsolescent AMX-30s. As a result, Saudi Arabia relies heavily on its 450 M-60A3s. This is still a significant amount of armor, but it is dispersed over much of the Kingdom, and Saudi Arabia lacks the training, manpower quality, sustainability, and C^4I/SR capabilities for effective, aggressive maneuver warfare and forward defense.

A force of five Iraqi divisions would compare favorably with four Kuwaiti brigades. However, only one of those brigades would be combat-ready, and total forward-deployed U.S. strength normally does not include a single forward-deployed land brigade. The Saudi forces at Hafr al Batin are at most the equivalent of two combat-effective brigades, which would probably take two weeks to fully deploy forward to the Kuwait and Saudi borders in sustainable, combat-ready form. The so-called Gulf Cooperation Council (GCC) rapid deployment force is largely a political faction with no meaningful real-world combat capability against Iraqi heavy divisions. Moreover, the new agreements that were signed in 2000 and 2001 to strengthen this force will do nothing substantive to change what is little more than a military façade.

Delays in U.S. power projection capability would inevitably limit U.S. ability to exploit its advantages in military technology and the land elements of the "revolution in military affairs." The United States has elements of one heavy brigade pre-positioned in Kuwait, but it takes at least 14–21 days to fully man, deploy, and sustain this brigade. The U.S. Army can deploy another two relatively light brigades in fully combat-ready form in 18–30 days, but the brigade set pre-positioned in Qatar would take several weeks to deploy to the Kuwaiti border area, and the division support set pre-positioned in Qatar could not deploy in fully combat-effective form until M+27 to M+35. The U.S. Army brigade pre-positioned on ships near Diego Garcia would take nearly a month to deploy in sustainable combat form.

The U.S. Marine Corps has another light division equivalent and air wing that it could deploy as a Marine Expeditionary Force, but it too would take at least three weeks to fully deploy. It would also lack heavy armor and artillery. Some aspects of Marine Corps readiness have been seriously underfunded in recent years. Although this is being corrected, it might still affect some aspects of combat capability.

As a result, a Saudi/U.S.-led coalition's ability to deal with a sudden Iraqi attack on Kuwait is likely to depend on U.S. ability to mass offensive air and missile power and use it immediately. The United States would need to act against Iraq the moment major troop movements began and do so without first seeking to win air superiority or air supremacy. It will also depend on U.S. willingness and ability to couple strikes against Iraqi leadership and strategic targets to this offensive in an effort to force Iraq to halt its offensive, as well as U.S. ability to deter, defend, and retaliate against any Iraqi use of weapons of mass destruction.

Much will still depend on Saudi Arabia and the other Gulf states. To be fully effective, the United States will require the full support of Saudi Arabia in committing its army and air force to the defense of Kuwait and the Saudi border area. It will depend on the Kingdom, Bahrain, and the other southern Gulf countries to assist in the deployment and basing of U.S. forces in the region. Additionally, the United States will also require immediate Kuwaiti willingness to allow the United States and Saudi Arabia to employ force against Iraq before its forces can deploy to the Kuwaiti border area.

Even then, preventing an Iraqi occupation of Kuwait City could be a difficult task if Iraq is willing to absorb very high levels of damage done by U.S. and allied air and missile power. In a worst-case scenario, a Saudi/U.S.-led coalition could be confronted with an asymmetric war in which Iraq ruthlessly exploited the suffering of the Kuwaiti people to force a halt to U.S. military action. Kuwaiti government security experts have, in fact, postulated a far worse case in which Iraq uses overt or covert attacks with biological weapons to effectively destroy Kuwait as a nation and create new facts on the ground.

As a result, Iraqi land forces might penetrate into and seize Kuwait City the city and take the Kuwaiti population as a hostage. USCENTCOM experts privately speculate that the United States would at best have a 50-50 chance of preventing Iraq from occupying Kuwait City. The only way that Iraqi forces could then be dislodged would be through a combination of another land buildup in Saudi Arabia by the United States and allied forces and a massive strategic/interdiction air campaign against targets on Iraqi territory.

The dilemma in any "second liberation" of Kuwait would then be U.S., Saudi, and Kuwaiti willingness to act in the face of potential massacres of Kuwaiti civilians versus the willingness of an Iraqi regime to accept massive damage to Iraq. It seems likely that the United States and Saudi Arabia would show the necessary ruthlessness if the Kuwaiti government supported such action. Oil is too strategically important to cede such a victory to a leader like Saddam Hussein.

Defending Kuwait will become an increasingly "close-run thing" if Iraq can escape the effect of sanctions and improve its ability to modernize and rebuild its war-fighting capability. There are a number of ways in which Iraq might then increase the challenge it could pose to U.S. capabilities and the "revolution in military affairs," without acquiring similar military technologies and capabilities:

- Iraq may somehow obtain nuclear weapons or demonstrate the possession of highly lethal biological weapons.

- The United States might be forced to reduce its forward presence and readiness in the Gulf to the point where it could not rapidly deploy airpower and/or reduce its overall power projection capabilities. This could occur either as a result of U.S. domestic political and funding issues or as a consequence of added Iranian and Iraqi success in their diplomatic campaigns to limit the U.S. role in the region.

- Iraq may choose a more limited and "acceptable" objective, like restoring its pre-Gulf War border or demanding access to Bubiyan, Warbah, the Kwar Abdullah, and the Gulf. This might make it harder for the United States to obtain support from its other regional allies and/or nations outside the Gulf.

- Improvements in relations between Iraq and Saudi Arabia might create a situation where Saudi Arabia may not immediately and fully support U.S. action and commit its own forces.

- The government of Kuwait may feel it faces so serious an increase in the Iraqi threat that it would refuse to accept the cost of continuing to fight in the face of ruthless Iraqi action against a "hostage" Kuwaiti people.

Iraq's Offensive Capabilities in Other Contingencies

The situation would be far more favorable to a Saudi/U.S.-led coalition in a contingency that did not involve Kuwait. Iraq has almost none of the assets necessary to win a naval-air battle against U.S. forces in the Gulf and has no prospect of acquiring these assets in the foreseeable future. It would have to rebuild, modernize, and massively expand both its regular navy and air force to levels of strength and capability it simply cannot hope to achieve for the next half decade. Alternatively, Iraq could develop its capabilities to deliver weapons of mass destruction to the point where it could support its conventional military capabilities with a threat that might seriously inhibit U.S. military action and/or the willingness of southern Gulf states to support the United States and provide air and naval facilities.

Unlike Iran, Iraq cannot conduct meaningful surface ship, naval air force, and amphibious operations. At present, the Iraqi navy is limited to conducting mine warfare, land-based anti-ship missile attacks, and surprise raids on offshore facilities. Its air force may be able to conduct limited anti-ship missile attacks using its Mirage F-1s, but would have to find a permissive environment to survive. Iraqi Mirage F-1s burdened with the AM-39 Exocet would be unlikely to survive Kuwaiti, Saudi, or Iranian air defenses, without a level of air escort capability that Iraq cannot currently provide.

As long as the United States has the ability to use its air and missile power to inflict enough strategic damage on Iraq to create a massive deterrent to any Iraqi escalation involving chemical or biological weapons and as long as the United States backs these capabilities with the ultimate threat of U.S. theater nuclear escalation, Iraq has little ability to intimidate its neighbors into accepting such operations. There is little near-term prospect that Iraq will develop enough power projection capability—and supporting power from its navy, air force, and weapons of mass destruction—to win any conflict in the southern Gulf in which it does not attack by land into Kuwait or across the Saudi border. The only exception would seem to be a case in which Iraq operated in support of a coup or uprising, or when Iraqi volunteers operated in southern Yemen in 1994. Any Iraqi attack on a southern Gulf state is also the contingency most likely to unite the United States and the southern Gulf states and would likely ensure the support of Europe and others for a strong U.S.–southern Gulf response.

This does not mean that Iraqi air and/or naval forces could not score some gains with a sudden, well-planned raid in the Gulf or challenge U.S. military capabilities in some ways. Iraq could not sustain any of these initial successes, however, and would probably accomplish nothing more than provoking a U.S., southern Gulf, or Iranian reaction that would far offset any advantages it could gain. The only exception might be a proxy unconventional or terrorist attack that would allow Iraq to preserve some degree of plausible deniability.

Iraq may also be able to achieve some of its objectives through intimidation or direct and indirect threats. Iraq's ability to provide such intimidation is now limited, but Iraq certainly understands that asymmetric warfare is a potential counter to U.S. superiority and the "revolution in military affairs," and it will seek to improve its capabilities once UN sanctions are lifted. In many cases, Iraq's neighbors may be willing to increasingly accommodate Iraq to some degree. This is particularly true of those states that see Iraq as a more serious threat—like Kuwait and Saudi Arabia.

Much will depend upon regional perceptions of the long-term resolve of the United States, the ability of the southern Gulf states to avoid major divisions, and the willingness of the southern Gulf states to show that they will support a firm U.S. response to Iraq, even at some risk. Much will also depend on the ability of Iraq's leadership to set achievable demands and avoid open confrontation. In broad terms, it seems likely that Iraq's ability to intimidate will slowly improve over time, but there is no way to predict how quickly or by how much.

CHAPTER 5

Iraq and Weapons of Mass Destruction

Iraq has a much more serious history of exploiting proliferation than Iran. It has seen proliferation as a counter to conventional superiority since the late 1960s. It sought weapons of mass destruction long before the Gulf War showed it what the "revolution in military affairs" and U.S. conventional superiority could accomplish. Since 1991, Iraq has been unable to obtain significant imports of conventional weapons and is incapable of producing its own. As a result, it is scarcely surprising that Iraq sees proliferation as its key potential method of countering the U.S. advantage in conventional forces and has been willing to pursue such options in the face of massive economic costs, UNSCOM and IAEA efforts to destroy its remaining capabilities, and the extension of UN sanctions.

The United States, Britain, and a number of other nations see Iraq's continuing efforts to acquire weapons of mass destruction as the most serious threat posed by the regime of Saddam Hussein. For 10 years they have sought to use UN sanctions to end these activities, and the United States has repeatedly struck Iraq since 1991 for violating the cease-fire and continuing to proliferate. The United States and Britain may eventually invade Iraq to remove the regime of Saddam Hussein, largely to put an end to Iraqi proliferation and the threat it poses to an area with more than 60 percent of the world's proven oil reserves.

This struggle over proliferation might best be described as a continuing low-intensity conflict that could suddenly become part of a major war with only limited warning rather than a possible contingency. Desert Fox has already shown that the United States and Britain will use major amounts of force to deal with Iraqi violations of the terms of the cease-fire in the Gulf War. Other struggles—such as that over the no-fly zones—could escalate to include Iraqi CBRN targets. Although a U.S.-led invasion of Iraq to remove the regime of Saddam Hussein may raise the most serious threat of extensive Iraqi use of CBRN weapons, it is scarcely the only contingency that could do so.

Iraqi Missile Developments and Possible Capabilities

Iraq continues to work on its Samoud ballistic missile system and other similar systems that supposedly have a range of fewer than 150 kilometers—although none of these systems are believed to be deployed and lack the range for effective strikes on most foreign cities and facilities. Iraq likely has at least 12–25 surviving Scud missile assemblies, however, and could have in excess of 40.

UNSCOM inspectors note that UNSCOM's claims to have identified 817 out of 819 Scud imports are extremely soft and may well have an error of 60 weapons and that no accurate count exists of Iraqi-produced components. This could give Iraq a range of 20–80 operational Scuds, and Iraq has shown in the past that it can produce its own TEL launchers. Iraq also continues development work on shorter-range missiles since missiles with ranges of 150 kilometers or fewer are permitted under the terms of the cease-fire.[22] UNSCOM made it clear in all of its reports, up through the final expulsion of its inspectors from Iraq, that Iraq was concealing the nature of its chemical and biological weapons effort and had systematically lied in every major disclosure report it had submitted to UNSCOM from the start to the end of the inspection effort.

Recent U.S. intelligence reporting provides the following assessment of Iraq's capabilities in this area. A CIA report in August 2000 summarized the state of Iraqi CBRN and missile development as follows:

- Since the Gulf War, Iraq has rebuilt key portions of its chemical production infrastructure for industrial and commercial use as well as its missile production facilities. It has attempted to purchase numerous dual-use items for, or under the guise of, legitimate civilian use. This equipment—in principle subject to UN scrutiny—also could be diverted for WMD purposes. Since the suspension of UN inspections in December 1998, the risk of diversion has increased.

- Following Desert Fox, Baghdad again instituted a reconstruction effort on those facilities destroyed by the U.S. bombing to include several critical missile production complexes and former dual-use chemical weapons (CW) production facilities. In addition, it appears to be installing or repairing dual-use equipment at CW-related facilities. Some of these facilities could be converted fairly quickly for the production of CW agents.

- Iraq continues to pursue the development of two SRBM systems that are not prohibited by the United Nations: the liquid-propellant Al Samoud and the solid-propellant Ababil-100. The Al Samoud is essentially a scaled-down Scud, and the program allows Baghdad to develop technological improvements that could be applied to a longer-range missile program. We believe that the Al Samoud missile, as designed, is capable of exceeding the UN-permitted 150-kilometer-range restriction with a potential operational range of about 180 kilometers. Personnel previously involved with the Condor II/Badr-2000 missile—which was largely destroyed during the Gulf War and eliminated by UNSCOM—are working on the Ababil-100 program. If economic sanctions against Iraq were lifted, Baghdad probably would attempt to convert these

---

22. An analysis by Charles Duelfer indicates that the count of 817 missile assemblies certified by UNSCOM includes 8 used in training before the Iran-Iraq War, 516 used during the Iran-Iraq War, 69 used in testing, 93 used in the Gulf War, 48 destroyed by UNSCOM, and 83 that Iraq asserted it had unilaterally destroyed. The count of those used in testing is particularly suspect.

efforts into longer-range missile systems, regardless of continuing UN monitoring and continuing restrictions on WMD and long-range missile programs.

A Department of Defense report in January 2001 reported that

- Iraq likely retains a limited number of launchers and SCUD-variant SRBMs capable of striking its neighbors, as well as the components and manufacturing means to assemble and produce others, anticipating the reestablishment of a long-range ballistic missile force sometime in the future. Baghdad likely also has warheads capable of delivering chemical or biological agents. Although Iraq's missile production infrastructure was damaged during the December 1998 strikes, Iraq retains domestic expertise and sufficient infrastructure to support most missile component production, with the exception of a few critical sub-elements.

- During 1999, Iraq continued to work on the two short-range ballistic missile systems that fall within the 150-kilometer range restriction imposed by the UN: the liquid-propellant Al Samoud and the solid-propellant Ababil-100. The Al Samoud is essentially a scaled-down SCUD, and work on it allows Baghdad to develop technological capabilities that could be applied to a longer-range missile program. We believe that the Al Samoud missile, as designed by the Iraqis, has an inherent potential to exceed the 150-kilometer range restriction imposed under UNSCR 687.

- Iraqi personnel involved with pre–Desert Storm ballistic missile efforts are working on the Ababil-100 SRBM program. Once economic sanctions against Iraq are lifted, unless restricted by future UN monitoring, Baghdad will probably begin converting these efforts into longer-range missile systems. Despite the damage done to Iraq's missile infrastructure during the Gulf War, Desert Fox, and subsequent UNSCOM activities, Iraq may have ambitions for longer-range missiles, including an ICBM.

- Iraq also has a variety of fighter aircraft, helicopters, artillery, and rockets available as potential means of delivery for NBC weapons, although their operational status is questionable owing to the cumulative effects of the UN arms embargo. However, Iraq has continued to work on its UAV program, which involves converting L-29 jet trainer aircraft originally acquired from Eastern Europe. These modified and refurbished L-29s may be intended for the delivery of chemical or biological agents. In the future, Iraq may try to use its research and development infrastructure to produce its own UAVs and cruise missiles or, should the UN arms embargo be lifted, it could try to purchase cruise missiles.

A CIA report issued in January 2002 stated that a military parade in December 2000 showcased Al Samoud missiles on new transporter-erector-launchers (TELs). The liquid-propellant Al-Samoud SRBM probably will be deployed soon. It projected future Iraqi capabilities as follows:

- Iraq is likely to use its experience with Scud technology to resume production of the pre–Gulf War 650-kilometer-range Al Hussein, the 900-kilometer-range Al

Abbas, or other Scud variants, and it could explore clustering and staging options to reach more distant targets. Iraq *could* resume Scud-variant production—with foreign assistance—quickly after UN prohibitions ended.

- With substantial foreign assistance, Baghdad *could* flight-test a domestic MRBM by mid-decade. This possibility presumes rapid erosion of UN prohibitions and Baghdad's willingness to risk detection of developmental steps, such as static engine testing, earlier. An MRBM flight test is *likely* by 2010. An imported MRBM *could* be flight-tested within months of acquisition.

- For the first several years after relief from UN prohibitions, Iraq probably will strive to reestablish its SRBM inventory to pre–Gulf War numbers, continue developing and deploying solid-propellant systems, and pursue MRBMs to keep pace with its neighbors. Once its regional security concerns are being addressed, Iraq may pursue a first-generation ICBM/SLV.

- Although Iraq *could* attempt before 2015 to test a rudimentary long-range missile based on its failed Al Abid SLV, such a missile almost certainly would fail. Iraq is unlikely to make such an attempt. After observing North Korean missile developments the past few years, Iraq would be more likely to pursue a three-stage TD-2 approach to an SLV or ICBM, which would be capable of delivering a nuclear weapon-sized payload to the United States.

- Some postulations for potential Iraqi ICBM/SLV concepts and timelines from the beginning of UN prohibition relief include the following: (1) If Iraq could buy a TD-2 from North Korea, it *could* have a launch capability within a year or two of a purchase; (2) it *could* develop and test a TD-1-type system within a few years; (3) if it acquired No Dongs from North Korea, it *could* test an ICBM within a few years of acquisition by clustering and staging the No Dongs—similar to the clustering of Scuds for the Al Abid SLV; (4) if Iraq bought TD-2 engines, it *could* test an ICBM within about five years of the acquisition, and (5) Iraq *could* develop and test a Taepo Dong-2-type system within about ten years of a decision to do so.

- Foreign assistance is key to Iraqi efforts to develop quickly longer-range missiles. Iraq relied on extensive foreign assistance before the Gulf War and will continue to seek foreign assistance to expand its current capabilities.

Missiles are scarcely the only threat in terms of delivery systems. Iraq has long worked on unmanned combat aerial vehicles (UCAVs) and drones and has experimented with the modification of L-29 trainers and MiG-21s in this role. It developed crude "sprayer" tanks and systems to deliver chemical and biological weapons using its aircraft and helicopters before the Gulf War and may since have developed more effective ways of releasing chemical and biological agents in "line-source" deliveries that would be an order of magnitude more lethal than release through conventional bombs and shells.

Iraqi CBRN Developments and Possible Capabilities

In spite of the Gulf War and nearly eight years of UNSCOM efforts before Iraq forced an end to the UN inspection effort, Iraq still presents a major threat in terms of proliferation. It is all too clear that Iraq may have increased this threat since active UNSCOM and IAEA efforts ended in December 1998. It is known to have continued to import precursors for chemical weapons and may have increased its holdings of biological growth agents. No one can dismiss the risk that Iraq does have weapons with very high real-world lethalities.

Recent U.S. intelligence reporting notes that it is not possible to collect detailed information on Iraq's CBRN programs, but that it almost certainly is advancing and is being given high priority. A CIA report in August 2000 summarized the state of biological weapons proliferation in Iraq as follows:[23]

■ Since Operation Desert Fox in December 1998, Baghdad has refused to allow United Nations inspectors into Iraq as required by Security Council Resolution 687. Although UN Security Council Resolution (UNSCR) 1284, adopted in December 1999, established a follow-on inspection regime to the United Nations Special Commission on Iraq (UNSCOM) in the form of the United Nations Monitoring, Verification, and Inspection Committee (UNMOVIC), there have been no UN inspections during this reporting period. Moreover, the automated video monitoring system installed by the UN at known and suspect WMD facilities in Iraq has been dismantled by the Iraqis. Having lost this on-the-ground access, it is difficult for the UN or the United States to accurately assess the current state of Iraq's WMD programs.

■ Since the Gulf War, Iraq has rebuilt key portions of its chemical production infrastructure for industrial and commercial use, as well as its missile production facilities. It has attempted to purchase numerous dual-use items for, or under the guise of, legitimate civilian use. This equipment—in principle subject to UN scrutiny—also could be diverted for WMD purposes. Since the suspension of UN inspections in December 1998, the risk of diversion has increased.

■ Following Desert Fox, Baghdad again instituted a reconstruction effort on those facilities destroyed by the U.S. bombing to include several critical missile production complexes and former dual-use CW production facilities. In addition, it appears to be installing or repairing dual-use equipment at CW-related facilities. Some of these facilities could be converted fairly quickly for production of CW agents.

■ UNSCOM reported to the Security Council in December 1998 that Iraq continued to withhold information related to its CW and biological weapons (BW) programs. For example, Baghdad seized from UNSCOM inspectors an air force

---

23. CIA, August 10, 2000, Unclassified Report to Congress on the Acquisition of Technology Relating to Weapons of Mass Destruction and Advanced Conventional Munitions, 1 July through 31 December 1999, Internet edition.

document discovered by UNSCOM that indicated that Iraq had not consumed as many CW munitions during the Iran-Iraq War in the 1980s as had been declared by Baghdad. This discrepancy indicates that Iraq may have an additional 6,000 CW munitions hidden.

■ We do not have any direct evidence that Iraq has used the period since Desert Fox to reconstitute its WMD programs, although given its past behavior, this type of activity must be regarded as likely. We assess that since the suspension of UN inspections in December of 1998, Baghdad has had the capability to reinitiate both its CW and BW programs within a few weeks to months, but without an inspection monitoring program, it is difficult to determine if Iraq has done so. We know, however, that Iraq has continued to work on its unmanned aerial vehicle program, which involves converting L-29 jet trainer aircraft originally acquired from Eastern Europe. These modified and refurbished L-29s are believed to be intended for delivery of chemical or biological agents.

A Department of Defense report—*Proliferation: Threat and Response*, issued in January 2001 by the secretary's office—stated that

Iraq's continued refusal to disclose fully the extent of its biological program suggests that Baghdad retains a biological warfare capability, despite its membership in the BWC [Biological Weapons Convention]. After four-and-one-half years of claiming that it had conducted only "defensive research" on biological weapons Iraq declared reluctantly, in 1995, that it had produced approximately 30,000 liters of bulk biological agents and/or filled munitions. Iraq admitted that it produced anthrax, botulinum toxins, and aflatoxins and that it prepared biological agent–filled munitions, including missile warheads and aerial bombs. However, UNSCOM believed that Iraq had produced substantially greater amounts than it has admitted—three to four times greater.

Iraq also admitted that, during the Persian Gulf War, it had deployed biological agent–filled munitions to airfields and that these weapons were intended for use against Israel and coalition forces in Saudi Arabia. Iraq stated that it destroyed all of these agents and munitions in 1991, but it has provided insufficient credible evidence to support this claim.

The UN believes that Baghdad has the ability to reconstitute its biological warfare capabilities within a few weeks or months, and, in the absence of UNSCOM inspections and monitoring during 1999 and 2000, we are concerned that Baghdad again may have produced some biological warfare agents.

Director of Central Intelligence George J. Tenet's February 6, 2002, testimony before the Senate Select Committee on Intelligence stated that "Iraq continues to build and expand an infrastructure capable of producing WMD. Baghdad is expanding its civilian chemical industry in ways that could be diverted quickly to CW production. We believe it also maintains an active and capable BW program; Iraq told UNSCOM it had worked with several BW agents."

John R. Bolton, under secretary for arms control and international security, described Iraq's status as follows in a speech on May 6, 2002: "Foremost is Iraq. Although it became a signatory to the BWC in 1972 and became a State Party in 1991, Iraq has developed, produced, and stockpiled biological warfare agents and weapons. The United States strongly suspects that Iraq has taken advantage of more than three years of no UN inspections to improve all phases of its offensive BW program. Iraq also has developed, produced, and stockpiled chemical weapons, and shown a continuing interest in developing nuclear weapons and longer range missiles."

Several senior UNSCOM inspectors believe that Iraq created new parallel chemical and biological weapons design efforts that were unrelated to its prewar efforts no later than 1995 and may have been able to develop better VX weapons, more lethal forms of anthrax and other noninfectious agents, and possibly weaponize smallpox. Once again, Iraq has had strong incentives to correct the problems in its previous CBRN weapons, but experts are deeply divided over the probability that Iraq has done so.

Much depends on how well Iraq has organized its CBRN forces and weaponized its chemical and biological agents. Virtually nothing is known in the unclassified literature about the Iraqi process since 1991 in this latter area, which can affect the real-world lethality of chemical and biological warheads, bombs, munitions, and sprayers by up to two orders of magnitude.

Iraq developed effective 155-mm artillery and 122-mm multiple rocket rounds for the delivery of chemical weapons during the Iran-Iraq War and could probably modify such technology to deliver biological weapons. The effective use of chemical weapons armed with artillery and multiple rocket rounds against large enemy ground forces does require an extensive inventory of munitions, however, even in using VX-gas. It is unclear that Iraq could conceal the production, deployment, and training for an operation of this scale. The delivery of biological agents using such weapons would present two critical problems: The effects would probably only develop after the battle was over, and there would be a serious risk of secondary effects if the agent blew back over Iraqi troops and civilian areas. The use of such attacks cannot be ruled out, however, particularly as a last extreme, and the troops firing such weapons would not have to be informed of such risks.

Iraq has had cluster bomb technology since the Iran-Iraq War and has long had the theoretical engineering capability to use nonexplosive release mechanisms like airbags to release chemical and biological munitions. Before the Gulf War, Iraq developed crude parachute release designs for its missile warheads, systems that would be substantially more effective than the primitive contact fuse warheads and bombs it had at the time of the war and that might well have produced negligible weapons effects if they had ever been used.

Iraq must realize that the crude contact fusing, and chemical/biological warhead/bomb designs, it had at the time of the Gulf War drastically limited the effectiveness of its CBRN weapons. Iraq has had strong incentives to correct these problems for more than a decade, and the development of parachute release weapons is only moderately challenging. Iraq has also had a decade to adapt nondestructive dissemination technology like airbags. Nevertheless, experts are deeply divided over Iraq's systems integration and engineering skill and the probability that Iraq has developed lethal missile warheads.

There is broad agreement among experts that Iraq has probably developed effective sprayer and line-source delivery technology since the Gulf War. This is the most lethal way to deliver chemical and biological weapons and is far more effective than using even advanced missile warheads. Iraq also experimented at the time of the Gulf War with using aircraft like the Czech L-29 trainer as a remotely piloted drone to carry out such deliveries at long ranges, and U.S. forces were deeply concerned that Iraq might be using its UAVs for such missions early in the Gulf War. The use of fighters, helicopters, and drones for such missions requires relatively large aircraft, and they would be vulnerable to air defenses. It is at least possible, however, that Iraq could use its best strike aircraft to fly a one-way mission and succeed in penetrating deep into southern Gulf, Turkish, and Kurdish territory or the rear area of U.S.-led coalition ground forces. It is also possible that Iraq might be able to use drones, UAV, or modified fighters, a global positioning (or GPS) guidance system, and earth-hugging flight profiles to create the equivalent of cruise missiles for such missions with sufficient accuracy and reliability to attack city-sized targets at long ranges.

Similar critical uncertainties exist in other areas of Iraqi CBRN war fighting. Several UNSCOM inspectors believe that Iraq lied about its ability to produce a stable form of persistent VX nerve gas during the time Iraq was still under inspection, just as it had lied earlier about weaponizing of VX. Iraq's mustard gas inventory proved to be highly stable during the period of inspection, and it seems likely that Iraq now has both stable nonpersistent and persistent nerve gas. Iraq is known to have continued to smuggle in precursor chemicals during the inspection period and since 1998. Persistent VX would probably be at least 10 times more lethal than anything Iraq used in the Iraq-Iraq War or against its Kurds.

Iraq has experimented with the conversion of biological agents into dry, coated micropowders that can be lethal to two orders of magnitude or more versus slurries of wet agents. At least in the case of the most lethal, advanced weaponized forms of dry-storable anthrax—such biological weapons can achieve the lethality of simple nuclear fission weapons. They can have far more immunity to heat and sunlight, disseminate without clumping, and are extremely lethal when inhaled. They can be nonexplosively disseminated with airbag technology and are far better suited to use in bombs, missile warheads, and covert attacks. Similarly, little is known about any Iraqi advances in sprayer and line-source delivery technology, and in tailoring chemical/biological (CB) agents to make them more effective in such delivery profiles. Contrary to some literature, truly effective line-source and sprayer delivery is a complex engineering problem involving both the agent and delivery system.

The greatest single unknown, in terms of Iraqi capability to use biological agents, consists of infectious agents like smallpox and plague. Iraq was one of the last countries to have a natural outbreak of smallpox and may well have the culture. Smallpox is easy to reproduce in a small facility and is infectious enough so agents willing to commit suicide or individuals who are unwittingly exposed could create serious corridors of infection. The long period between exposure and symptoms deprives such agents of immediate impact in war-fighting scenarios, but they could be used in port, airbase, or rear areas during the staging of enemy forces with limited risk because Iraq's borders would be sealed. Infiltrating the agent into Turkey, southern Gulf states, Israel, or the United States and UK would be an option; as is sending in exposed unwitting or deliberately infected individuals. No meaningful capability now exists to screen for the agent or exposed individuals, and agents carrying smallpox agent could be immunized, as could those infecting unwitting subjects.

IAEA and U.S. intelligence experts privately put little or no faith in the claims of various Iraqi defectors that Iraq retains the ability to make fissile material, has extensive covert fissile material production facilities, and has workable bomb designs small enough to be used in missile warheads. IAEA experts note that the Iraqi diffusion effort was never effective, that the Calutron designs fell far short of meeting specification, that Iraq's centrifuge designs proved to be far less effective during laboratory review than they initially estimated, and that Iraq does not seem to have understood the technical problems in using centrifuges to enrich fissile material beyond 90 percent. They note that cascades of centrifuges are relatively easy to conceal in multistory buildings, but that Iraq is extremely dependent on imports to create such a facility and would probably need outside technical support.

Iraq did, however, have at least two workable fissile weapon implosion designs that could be used in large bombs at the time of the Gulf War, had solved the technical problems in making and triggering high explosive lenses for nuclear weapons, and had workable neutron initiators. If it could obtain fissile material, it could probably make a large explosive device relatively quickly, but not fit one to a missile warhead or build a bomb that any of its aircraft other than its bombers and MiG-24s could deliver at long distances, particularly in low-altitude penetration missions. Iraq might be much more successful in arming any actual nuclear weapon it could obtain, particularly because of the relatively crude PAL systems fitted to many FSU weapons and the duplicative code sequences used to arm them.

Iraq has shown both that it can disperse and conceal and that it is willing to take serious risks in doing so in spite of the centralized nature of the regime. During the Gulf War, Iraq was willing to place large numbers of chemical weapons under the control of its regular army forces, although biological weapons and missiles were placed under the control of special units of the Republican Guard, which seem to have had a significant element of Iraqi security forces. Iraq also showed during the Gulf War that it could disseminate chemical weapons (and possibly biological weapons) over a wide area without detection by coalition forces. Coalition intelligence and targeting of such weapons stocks was a near total failure through the end of the war, and advancing forces sometimes had to be warned of the existence of stockpiles of chemical weapons by surrendering Iraqi officers. Iraq mixed chemical and conventional munitions stockpiles without special security precautions and even dispersed unguarded weapons at unused airstrips for possible arming in a last-ditch emergency.

A number of experts believe Iraq could disperse most of its covert biological production on warning or under attack. Iraq is known to have mobile laboratories and storage equipment and to have developed advanced techniques for rapid equipment and material movement during the time of UN inspection. It is not known whether Iraq has developed special survivable communications for such dispersal efforts or exactly who would control such units and how loyal they would be under extreme conditions—particularly knowing the probable level of reprisals both in terms of the level of attacks on Iraq and future treatment of war criminals. Regimes like Iraq's do, however, have a long history of successfully indoctrinating and lying to carefully selected "loyalist" units. Such units can now also make use of GPS rather than pre-surveyed sites and may well be able to make use of GPS for preplanned targeting or to change targeting in the field. This could increase the dispersal area and the effectiveness with which an Iraqi force would be able to target cities and fixed facilities at long ranges.

Current War-fighting Capability "Guesstimates"

Possible U.S. Response

Cumulatively, these uncertainties make it impossible to do more than guess at Iraq's war-fighting capabilities. As such a guesstimate, Iraq's present holdings of delivery systems and chemical and biological weapons seem most likely to be so limited in technology and operational lethality that they do not severely constrain U.S. freedom of action or seriously intimidate Iraq's neighbors.

Barring classified intelligence to the contrary, Iraqi CBRN capabilities must be taken seriously, but do not seem great enough to change U.S., British, Iranian, Israeli, Saudi and/or southern Gulf perceptions of risk to the point where they would limit or paralyze military action against Iraq by a U.S.-led coalition or prevent large-scale Israeli strikes on Iraq.

Iraq has not fired any Scud variants in nearly 12 years. There are no public reports that it has tested dry-storable biological weapons or has made major advances in its weaponization of nerve gas. Furthermore, it seems unlikely that Iraq can openly build up major production and deployment capabilities without them being detected and targeted and without provoking strong U.S. counterproliferation programs, including preemptive or retaliatory strike capabilities.

Nevertheless, Iraq's possession of even moderately effective CBRN weapons must affect other aspects of U.S., British, southern Gulf, and Israeli perceptions of the risks inherent in attacking Iraq. President Bush has already made it clear that the United States might well make maximum use of its advanced intelligence, surveillance, and reconnaissance (ISR) capabilities, and air and missile power to carry out a massive preemptive strike on Iraq's CBRN and delivery capabilities at the first sign of any major crisis or as a prelude to an invasion to overthrow Saddam.[24] Such weapons create a strong incentive for preemption even in "peacetime conditions" *if* (1) they can be targeted with sufficient reliability and depth of coverage, (2) the United States and its allies are confident the resulting strikes would do sufficient

---

24. According to some reports, General Tommy Franks, the commander of USCENTCOM, has made such preemptive strikes part of his contingency planning. See John Hendren, "In Iraq, U.S. Faces New Dynamics," *Los Angeles Times*, July 6, 2002, p. 1.

damage to offset the risk of Iraq lashing out with its surviving weapons, (3) the United States is confident any secondary effects in terms of Iraqi civilian casualties would be limited, and (4) the United States is convinced it can show the world that Iraq was in violation of the UN cease-fire. Preemption might also take place regardless of these risks—if the United States was convinced that Iraq was making preparations to use such weapons or had dispersed a force for their possible delivery.

It should be noted in this regard that the physical destruction of stored or dispersed chemical and biological facilities and munitions stored on the ground presents only a limited risk of major collateral damage and secondary civilian casualties unless the weapons are in densely populated areas. No one can disprove the idea of trace effects from such explosions, such as those associated with Gulf War syndrome, but the probabilities are limited.

Any major punitive U.S. and British attack on Iraq would almost certainly target suspect Iraqi CBRN and delivery facilities immediately at the beginning of such an attack. So would any U.S.-led coalition attack designed to remove Saddam from power. Some experts argue this would trigger an Iraqi response when Iraq might otherwise not use its CBRN forces and ride out a conflict. Most experts argue, however, that Iraq is unlikely to reveal it has such weapons in a punitive attack, trying to preserve what it can, and would use such weapons in any case in any attack large enough to threaten the regime.

As has been touched upon earlier, it is impossible to estimate the success of such U.S. attacks or how much U.S. ISR and targeting capability against Iraqi CBRN forces has actually improved since Desert Fox. Waiting for enemy assets to be dispersed can also create an impossible tactical burden. Although the Bush administration has talked about preemption, talk about preemption is much cheaper than acquiring the ability to actually execute it.[25] Iraq has had decades in which to improve its use of deception, dispersal, decoys, and other countermeasures to U.S. ISR and surveillance capabilities.

In spite of some wartime claims to the contrary, the United States was unable to detect and target most Iraqi CBRN and missile capabilities during the Gulf War. During the Gulf War, the United States flew some 2,400 sorties searching for and trying to strike at dispersed Iraqi Scud missiles. On some 42 occasions, U.S. aircraft spotted a launch plume and made 8 actual attacks. Nevertheless, neither coalition airpower nor Special Forces damaged a single Scud, and Iraq was able to fire some 88 Scuds against Israel and Saudi Arabia.[26] Iraq also successfully dispersed its missiles and bombs to create a crude retaliatory strike capability to deliver CB weapons if the regime collapsed or lost the ability to command Iraq forces. It took major

---

25. For a discussion of some of these issues, see Christopher J. Bowie, "Destroying Mobile Ground Targets in an Anti-Access Environment," Analysis Center Papers, Northrup Grumman, December 2001; and Vernon Loeb, "U.S. Gains in Attacking Mobile Arms," *Washington Post*, July 5, 2002, p. A-14.

26. Barry Watts, "Effects and Effectiveness," *Gulf War Air Power Survey,* vol. 2 (Washington, D.C.: U.S. Government Printing Office, 1993), p. 335; Christopher J. Bowie, "Destroying Mobile Ground Targets in an Anti-Access Environment," Northrup Grumman Analysis Center Paper, Washington, D.C., December 2001, p. 3.

risks in collocating CB and conventional weapons and in dispersing such weapons without security protection.

The massive U.S. intelligence and air strike effort following the beginning of Iraqi missile strikes on Saudi Arabia and Israel failed to characterize the changes in Iraqi facilities and capabilities made during the course of the war and had no meaningful successes against dispersed missiles. The diversion of large amounts of U.S. targeting and air assets may have degraded Iraqi operations, but had little actual lethality. U.S. and British Special Forces failed to locate and target Iraqi missiles and CBRN weapons.

The U.S. and British air and missile strikes during Desert Fox seem to have been no more successful. The United States failed to find and strike significant Iraqi CBRN facilities. As a result, Desert Fox at most had only a few successes in hitting large Iraqi missile production facilities, and these were overt targets because they were permitted under the terms of the UN cease-fire. It is unclear that other raids had any useful impact, particularly because most critical equipment could be rapidly dispersed or sheltered. There seem to be good reasons why the U.S. military has never released any meaningful damage assessment data on Desert Fox.

U.S. ISR capabilities have changed significantly in years following the Gulf War, and even since Desert Fox. Even so, they have their limits. It is unlikely that the United States can count on detecting and accurately targeting most of a mobile Iraqi launch on warning (LOW), launch under attack (LUA), or retaliatory force for the delivery of CBRN weapons once it is deployed. The United States might well not detect the initial deployment of such a capability unless Iraq chose to signal this for deterrent purposes.

Proliferation and CBRN threats do fundamentally change the risks and values of war. Proliferators give their enemies the right to preemption and first strikes simply by proliferating, and the axiom that the only way to go to war with the United States is with the possession of nuclear weapons is one the United States must aggressively counter, regardless of whether a nation or terrorist movement is involved. Waiting for enemy assets to be dispersed can also create an impossible tactical burden.

The threat of biological warfare is particularly serious, and the United States and its allies need to rethink internal security planning, public health response, and defense efforts to deal with the broad range of CBRN threats. The failure of members of the European Union to cooperate fully with Britain in the treatment of hoof and mouth disease and "mad cow" disease is almost a model of how not to deal with the need for such cooperation and serves as a warning about how much more effort is needed to address both time-urgent tactical and the broad spectrum of global threats.

That said, it is one thing to have a doctrine and plans and quite another to have a capability. Any form of attack on CBRN and their delivery system assets must involve meaningful targeting capability, the proper weapons and destructive means, and careful consideration of civilian and could not carry out a successful attack on Iraq's CBRN assets at either the time of the Gulf War or Desert Fox. It had no idea of what to target at the beginning of the Afghan conflict.

Preemption—and any other form of strikes—will also have much more limited effectiveness if Iraq has created some kind of well-concealed LOW force before the strikes begin, or if Iraq deployed one the moment it detects that the United States is preparing to launch a preemptive strike on Iraq's CBRN and missile capabilities or is preparing a major land attack and coalition effort to overthrow the ruling regime and/or occupy the country. No credible unclassified reports have yet surfaced that Iraq has such a capability in place. However, it is possible that such a covert capability does exist.

The key question is whether U.S. intelligence and air strike capabilities may have advanced to the point where the United States might well destroy many important fixed equipment items and facilities and disrupt some aspects of Iraqi operations. Continuing U.S. and British strikes may be able to severely limit or even suppress Iraqi ability to sustain CBRN operations over time—if the United States organized and sustained a major effort to provide continuing surveillance and strike capability over probable launch areas and any suspected Iraqi CBRN facilities and infrastructure.

Unfortunately, it is less clear that U.S. or British Special Forces have made effective efforts to improve their wide area coverage to support such an air-cruise missile strike effort. The real-world capabilities of the improved Patriot and Arrow also present major uncertainties about the level of anti-ballistic missile (ATBM) defense that would be available, and much would depend on the readiness and deployment of such ATBM forces.[27]

Offense is scarcely the only defense. U.S. missile launch detection, launch point targeting, and probable impact point prediction capabilities have improved significantly since the Gulf War, although much more advanced systems will be deployed after 2010 that will improve key aspects of missile defense and targeting. Steady improvements in the U.S. Patriot have improved its ballistic and cruise missile kill capabilities, particularly against the Scud-type missiles that Iraq can deploy, but the Patriot remains basically a point defense system in dealing with ballistic missiles, and much would depend on where it was deployed at the time of an attack.

It seems likely, therefore, that Iraq could succeed in launching some CBRN strikes against U.S. coalition forces, targets in neighboring states, and/or Israel. If so, Iraq would face the problem of using weapons whose accuracy and lethality it has had no way to operationally test in any realistic way. Iraq would not be firing blind or be totally ignorant of the possible lethality of its weapons, but it would not have any basis for making reliable judgments about how many weapons would fully function, their operational accuracy, the effectiveness of its long-range targeting, or the lethality of the weapon once it hit. It would also have to rely on satellite TV and other outside media for damage assessment.

At the same time, targeted forces and countries would be confronted with CB agents of unknown character, weaponization quality, and operational lethality. As a result, the defender could only characterize the weapon after it struck, which could take hours or days in the case of biological weapons. At present, even U.S. forces

---

27. Press reports that SAS forces could locate and destroy Iraqi BW facilities seem little more than speculation (*Times* [London], July 12, 2002, p. 1).

would only be able to firmly characterize dissemination by observing the lethal effects, and the Gulf War has shown that no military power is yet ready to estimate and counter the low-level and lingering effects of CB weapons against its forces. In spite of some pseudoscientific modeling efforts and post-action studies of Iraqi use of CB weapons, this is even more true of the assessment of the effects of such weapons against civilian targets—where the psychological, political, disruptive, and economic effects may in any case be more important than actual short- or long-term lethality.

This situation is likely to have the following war-fighting effects:

- In the best case, U.S. coalition forces and neighboring states could easily ride out a *current* Iraqi CBRN resulting attack; it simply would not be lethal enough to force massive retaliation.

- In the more likely case, the Iraqi attack would at least be politically successful enough to force the same major diversion of U.S. and other air strike and intelligence assets as during the Gulf War. This would not save the Iraqi regime, but does mean the United States must size its air and missile forces to cover this contingency. This would require major theater-wide air capabilities in excess of those needed for conventional war fighting.

- The United States and other defenders must plan to deploy the best available ATBM defenses and suitable passive defenses to deal with CB attacks on ports, airfields, and major U.S. staging facilities, as well as on allied cities and key oil facilities. Although highly lethal Iraqi attacks now seem unlikely, they are possible. (And, Iraqi capabilities are likely to steadily increase with time.)

- In the *current* worst case, the United States and its allies could take serious—if scarcely crippling—casualties. This could force the United States to threaten Iraq with a massive response to any Iraqi use of CBRN weapons and then execute it. The question then would be whether any conventional destruction of Iraq's leadership, military, economic, and infrastructure targets would be rapid and drastic enough to persuade the loyalist elements operating the Iraqi CBRN force to stop striking. The same question would apply to any U.S. threat to use nuclear weapons, although such threats seem to have had some effect during the Gulf War.

- The outlying version of the worst case is that Saddam should inflict serious enough damage on U.S. or allied forces, or regional targets, for the United States to engage in nuclear escalation. It is at least possible that such escalation might be the only way to confront the Iraqi military with sufficient reason to cease obeying orders to use CBRN weapon in a contingency where the existence of Saddam's regime was threatened.

As has been touched upon earlier, the key wild cards in this list of conclusions are (1) the assumption that Iraq has no nuclear weapons and no combination of weaponized biological agents and delivery systems so deadly that they could achieve "nuclear" or "strategic" lethalities and (2) Iraqi ability and willingness to use infectious weapons like smallpox and plague.

There also is no expert agreement about Iraqi willingness to escalate and how loyal and ready the Iraqi troops actually using such weapons would be in the face of threats to massively attack Iraq in response and treat them as war criminals. Deterrence is easy to postulate or deny, but its effectiveness is purely speculative. A few experts also argue that Saddam Hussein might launch on warning or under attack for several reasons: (1) he believes that the United States and its allies would be most vulnerable to massive casualties and find it hardest to sustain an offensive if they took such casualties early in a war; (2) he would have the tightest control over the forces involved and the most reliable communications; (3) the threat of follow-on attacks would be credible; and (4) he would have the largest number of surviving forces.

Israeli Response

It is dangerous to view the Iraqi threat to Israel only in terms of Iraq's possible use of missile strikes and CBRN weapons against Israel to try to end Arab support for some U.S.-led effort to overthrow Saddam Hussein. Iraq has used political support of the Palestinian cause as a political weapon since the late 1980s and has backed the Second Intifada as a useful tool in winning Arab popular support and influencing other Arab regimes. The $25,000 it pays directly to the families of Palestinian suicide bombers is scarcely an act of altruism. Israel is already a political and diplomatic weapon to prevent Arab support for any invasion of Iraq, and Iraq is likely to continue to exploit every opportunity to use this weapon.

According to expert reports, Israel sees an Iraqi missile attack on Israel as an inevitable part of any major U.S.-led invasion to overthrow Saddam's regime and believes such an attack might well use CBRN weapons. It feels it has no choice other than to support such an attack because any effort to oppose it or stand aside would be futile and simply result in the growth of steadily worse Iraqi threats even if the United States did not attack.

Israel has also concluded that the credibility of its deterrent would be undermined if it rode out another series of such attacks, as it did during the Gulf War. As a result, Israel would launch a major counterstrike in the event of another round of missile strikes. The degree to which it might or might not resort to nuclear escalation in the face of lethal CBRN strikes on an Israeli city or major area target is a subject IDF officers and Israeli officials will not discuss except on a personal basis and in the most speculative terms.

Compared with the United States, Israel has limited intelligence, surveillance, and targeting capabilities to cover all of Iraq—although improvements to its intelligence satellites are changing this situation and its intelligence and targeting capabilities are far better than in 1991. Israel did conduct extensive exercises to examine its options for such attacks in 2002 and engaged in extensive strategic planning talks to consider various contingencies and their political and military consequences.

Israel does have military limits. Its air force is capable of effective long-range strikes against known targets, but cannot sustain a loitering or "kill box"–type presence to seek out difficult mobile or concealed targets or try to suppress Iraqi missile firings by sustaining a presence over launch areas. Israel has only limited ISR capabilities to target dispersed and covert Iraqi CBRN forces.

In spite of various claims in the past, Israeli Special Forces also have little real-world capability to assist in targeting and destroying Iraqi forces that are dispersed over wide areas, particularly when Iraq is likely to have large numbers of decoys and rapid movement. Its land and air forces would also have to move over or through Jordan.

Israel does have active Arrow missile defenses, which have more area coverage than the U.S. Patriot. U.S. missile launch detection, launch point targeting, and probable impact point prediction data would be provided to Israel as well as to the Arab allies of the United States, and possibly Israel would get early warning data from Jordan—whose radar capabilities have improved in recent years. However, the Arrow ATBM now has more value as a deterrent against missile strikes than as a proven defense capability. The Arrow test program has been far too limited, narrow in coverage, and rushed to make a convincing war-fighting case for the system.

The most probable Israeli reaction to a new round of Iraqi missile attacks would be as follows:

- In the best case, Israel could easily ride out the resulting attack; it simply would not be lethal enough to force massive retaliation. In such a case, Israel might carry out major conventional strikes against critical Iraqi military or economic targets to show its resolve. The impact this would actually have on the Arab world is easy to exaggerate. It would be carried out in the context of massive, ongoing U.S.-led coalition air operations and might well appear to be little more than military "noise" in the midst of much larger ongoing coalition operations. Although such an Israeli role might well anger many in the Arab world, it may not have much real-world impact on the actions of key Arab governments. It seems just as likely that Israeli military action would increase the pressure of Arab governments on the United States to reach a rapid and decisive conclusion, as it would actually inhibit operations.

- In the more likely case, the Iraqi attack would not be lethal enough to kill large numbers of Israelis or pose an existential threat. Israel would then have to decide whether to issue nuclear threats as well as execute conventional strikes on Iraq. Much would depend on how quickly and confidently Israel could characterize the nature and lethality of the Iraqi hits on Israel.

- In the worst case, Israel would face what could become a cumulative existential threat to key urban areas, like Tel Aviv and Haifa. Under these conditions, it might openly declare its nuclear deterrent and threaten nuclear retaliation against Iraqi cities and military forces in an effort to halt Iraqi action. If Iraq should succeed in delivering extremely lethal biological agents against an Israeli city, Israel would probably massively retaliate with nuclear ground bursts against every Iraqi city not already occupied by U.S.-led coalition forces. This could destroy Iraq as a state. Israel would also probably then posture itself for hair trigger massive retaliation against any Syrian or Palestinian effort to exploit the Iraqi strikes.

There are several wild cards here. One is infiltration into Israel of knowing or unwitting agents either spreading an infectious agent by contact or carrying one for covert dissemination. Another is that Israel has enough intelligence to risk a decapitation attack on the Iraqi leadership rather than a more orthodox form of retaliation.

Jordan is caught in the middle of this potential struggle, and Jordanian officials are divided over whether Jordan should support a U.S.-led invasion to be on the winning side or resist any role in U.S. military action. They face a similar dilemma over cooperating with Israel in the event of an Iraqi missile attack because of the risk that Iraqi missiles might land on Jordan. In practice, King Abdullah and Jordanian officials tend to be more supportive of the West than the vast majority of the Jordanian people—whether Transjordanian or Palestinian.

This has led some experts to argue that Iraq might indirectly attack Israel during any missile attack or during a major conventional struggle by attacking the Hashemite regime. In such a scenario, Iraq might support assassination attempts on the King, royal family, and senior Jordanian officials. It might also inspire riots and major demonstrations or insist on moving forces into Jordan. This risk is compounded by the possibility the United States might use Jordan's Red Sea ports and common border with Iraq to stage a land attack from the West or seek air basing in Jordan. Iraq also knows that Israel is most likely to overfly Jordan if it retaliates for Iraqi missile strikes and has an incentive to try to involve Jordanian air defenses to try to block such Iraqi raids.

Turkish and Southern Gulf Response

Iraq used large numbers of Scuds to strike at Saudi Arabia during the Gulf War. As has been discussed earlier, it has a wide range of incentives to strike at those southern Gulf states that support, base, and stage U.S. and allied forces in any invasion of Iraq. This is a key reason the United States might have to devote major air assets to a "Scud hunt" in such a contingency, as well as rush in ATBM/aid defense units like the Patriot.

Iraq is extremely unlikely to use missiles and CBRN weapons to strike at Turkey unless Turkey actively supports a U.S.-led coalition. Even then it may be very reluctant to act. Turkey is scarcely likely to be passive if it is subject to such an attack. It has a major air force and has corps-level ground forces near the Iraqi border. The Turkish army has already moved into northern Iraq on several occasions to keep it from being a sanctuary for Turkish Kurd opposition forces, and one of these operations seems to have involved as many as 30,000 men. Few in the region see provoking the Turks as likely to result in successful intimidation rather than a massive military response.

Future Risks and Breakout Problems

One of the key questions affecting any military assessment of Iraq is what happens if Saddam stays in power, the United States does not take military action, and the present sanctions regime fails. If UN sanctions on Iraq are lifted or sharply weakened, Iraq may be able to rebuild its strategic delivery capabilities relatively quickly.

And any serious future conflict involving weapons of mass destruction could then have much more drastic consequences than seems likely to be the case today. This would be particularly true if Iraq could develop advanced biological weapons with near-nuclear lethality or assemble nuclear devices with weapons-grade fissile material bought from an outside source. There might be little or no warning of such strategic developments, and the United States might not be willing to counter by extending theater nuclear deterrence to protect its southern Gulf allies.

There are several other developments that might allow Iraq to use proliferation to pose a much more serious near-term threat to U.S. conventional capabilities in the region:

- *A successful Iraqi attempt to buy significant amounts of weapons-grade material.* This could allow Iraq to achieve a nuclear breakout capability in a matter of months. Both the United States and the region would find it much harder to adjust to such an Iraqi effort than to the slow development of nuclear weapons by creating fissile material within Iraq. It seems likely that the United States could deal with the situation by extending a nuclear umbrella over the Gulf, but even so, the southern Gulf states might be far more responsive to Iraqi pressure and intimidation. Most, after all, are so small that they are virtually "one bomb states."

- *A change in the U.S. and regional perception of biological weapons.* Biological weapons are now largely perceived as unproven systems of uncertain lethality. Regardless of their technical capabilities, they have little of the political impact that the possession of nuclear weapons has. Iraq might, however, conduct live animal tests to demonstrate that its biological weapons have near-nuclear lethality, or some other power might demonstrate their effectiveness in another conflict. The successful mass testing or use of biological weapons might produce a rapid "paradigm shift" in the perceived importance of such weapons and of Iraq's biological warfare programs.

- *Iraq might break out of UN sanctions and reveal a more substantial capability than now seems likely.* Paradoxically, such an Iraqi capability would help to legitimize Iran and Israel's nuclear, biological, and chemical programs and the escalation to the use of such weapons.

- *Iraq might use such weapons through proxies, or in covert attacks with some degree of plausible deniability.* Terrorism and unconventional warfare would be far more intimidating if they made use of weapons of mass destruction.

Iraq Uses Covert Action or a Terrorist/Extremist Proxy in Major Attacks against the United States, Britain, Israel, or a Gulf State

Opinions differ sharply as to Iraq's capability *and willingness* to carry out covert attacks or use terrorist and extremist movements as proxies. There are experts who believe that Iraq was directly involved in the first attack on the World Trade Center in 1993, played a role in the attack on the USAF barracks in Al Khobar, helped support Al Qaeda in the "9/11" attack on the World Trade Center and the Pentagon, and/or played a role in the anthrax attacks that followed.

No "smoking gun" has emerged in any of these cases, however, and the problems of proving a conspiracy took place are matched by the problems of proving a double negative—first, proving that a conspiracy did not take place and, second, proving that any credible conspiracy theory is the only possible explanation of the facts. In short, it may be equally possible to either convincingly prove that Iraq was involved in such conspiracies or that it was not.

The various branches of Iraqi intelligence do have a long history of overseas operations and ties to extremist groups. Iraq actively supported various extremist groups in the Gulf and the rest of the Middle East until the mid-1970s. Although it halted most such efforts after the Algiers Accords and sought the assistance of other Arab states in dealing with Iran from the mid-1970s to the time of the Gulf War, it did conduct covert operations in Kuwait during 1990 and carried out extensive infiltration operations across the Kuwaiti and Saudi borders after 1991. Iraqi intelligence may have been involved in an assassination plot against former President Bush.

The U.S. State Department reports that Iraq has provided bases to several terrorist groups including the Mujahedin-e-Khalq (MEK), the Kurdistan Workers' Party (PKK), the Palestine Liberation Front (PLF), and the Abu Nidal Organization (ANO). In 2001, the Popular Front for the Liberation of Palestine (PFLP) raised its profile in the West Bank and Gaza Strip by carrying out successful terrorist attacks against Israeli targets. In recognition of the PFLP's growing role, an Iraqi vice president met with former PFLP secretary general Habbash in Baghdad in January 2001 and expressed continued Iraqi support for the intifada. Following this meeting, a senior delegation from the PFLP met with an Iraqi deputy prime minister in September 2001. Iraq also continued to host other Palestinian rejectionist groups, including the Arab Liberation Front and the 15 May Organization.

Unlike Iran, however, Iraq has never demonstrated much capability to conduct "proxy wars" by training, arming, and funding Arab extremist movements. Iraq does sponsor some extremist and terrorist groups, but the end result has done little for Iraq. Iraq also lacks Iran's bases, training centers, and staging facilities in other countries and the political support of third nations, like the Sudan and Syria, that are close to the scene of such proxy conflicts. Similarly, Iraq can only hope to win proxy wars fought against vulnerable governments. Attempts to fight such wars will have little impact on a successful Arab-Israeli peace settlement or in sustaining civil conflict in the face of a government that demonstrates that it has the capacity to govern and deal with its social problems.

Iraq has some capability for information warfare and cyberterrorism, but it seems very unlikely that it is capable of advanced attacks on protected U.S. military and U.S. government systems. Iraq also probably has little capability to attack the U.S. private sector and the information systems of Gulf states. It is, however, steadily improving the defense of its own systems. Most are redundant, rely heavily on buried land-links and optical fibers, and are isolated from netted or open systems.

The best documented Iraqi intelligence operations, in recent years, have involved surveillance and attacks on opposition elements, various forms of money laundering and movement, and the support of Iraq's extensive network of clandestine purchasing offices. There are probably Iraqi agents and sleepers in all of the major Kurdish movements and in virtually every outside Iraqi opposition movement. Most such opposition groups seem to be totally transparent to Iraqi intelligence with the possible exception of those movements backed by Iran. The Iraqi purchasing and financial networks give Iraqi intelligence a significant presence in Europe and the Middle East, one that can easily move weapons and money to destinations other than Iraq.

Although reports of Iraqi intelligence contacts with Al Qaeda remain controversial, the fact remains that most Middle Eastern intelligence services maintain contact with a wide range of extremist and terrorist groups that they might arm, finance, and potentially use as proxies. This includes the intelligence services of every regional power friendly to the United States, as well as the more radical powers like Iran, Iraq, Libya, Syria, and the Sudan. Iraqi intelligence may have operational cells in countries like Yemen, as well as in the United States, Canada, and Europe.

As a result, Iraq might well be able to mount a covert or proxy attack if it chose to do so and might attempt an act of mass terrorism or use its weapons of mass destruction in such a way. Although some argue that Iraq would never turn CBRN weapons over to a terrorist or extremist movement because of the risk that they would be used against other targets, much would depend on the level of risk Iraq perceived or whether Saddam Hussein felt his regime was threatened or on the edge of destruction. It is also impossible to rule out possible Iraqi agents in place with cells designed to either use biological weapons or conduct some other dramatic form of attack. Similarly, Iraq might well calculate that it could ride out such attacks or preserve plausible deniability, given the wide range of possible extremist attackers, the past problems that the United States has had in identifying attackers, and the uncertain U.S. response to past terrorist attacks.

The most dangerous options involved would probably be biological warfare, barring the risk of some form of "loose nuke." Sabotage of civilian facilities, chemical terrorism, and radiological terrorism could produce serious casualties but not critical ones. The worst scenarios would involve the covert creation of capabilities in place to deliver significant amounts of dry, storable, coated micropowders of anthrax (slurries and wet agents would be difficult to handle and disseminate) or infectious agents like smallpox (Iraq was one of the last countries to have outbreaks of smallpox and may have a culture).

Any total collapse of the Arab-Israeli peace process or sign of instability in the Gulf's regimes might allow Iraq to use proxy wars more successfully. So would any unforeseen events that led to the creation of a radical Arab regime in Jordan and Egypt and a Syria that turned to Iraq for support. Iraq has a strong revanchist motive to use proxy warfare against Israel, Saudi Arabia, and the United States. The practical problem that Iraq faces will be to find a place and contingency where it could exploit such capabilities that offer more return than using proxies and allow Iraq to act at an acceptable level of risk at which the United States and its allies would not retaliate.

CHAPTER 6

Iraq versus the United States and a U.S.-led Coalition

A major U.S. military effort to overthrow Saddam Hussein's regime is perhaps the most complex and dangerous contingency that Iraq faces. The previous contingency analyses have already illustrated many of the issues that would be involved, but any such U.S. attack would have a different character from either the Gulf War or the U.S. and British military actions that have taken place as part of containment. Such an attack would be an "existential" attack on Saddam's regime and the one most likely to provoke extreme efforts and responses from Saddam and those around him. Actual U.S. military success that brought the regime to collapse or near collapse is also the case most likely to lead Iraq to employ CBRN weapons against foreign countries and forces.

Once again, however, there are several possible scenarios, and each imposes different strains on Iraqi capabilities. There also is no fixed level of force the United States would need to execute any given scenario nor would it need any fixed mix of allies and bases. Much depends on the level of risk the United States is willing to accept for itself and for its allies, the level of casualties it is willing to take and inflict, and its postwar approach to nation building.

Regardless of the scenario, conducting such a U.S. military operation and building the necessary regional and coalition support will not be easy. Although this analysis focuses on military, not political, issues, it is clear that the pressures created by existing U.S. military operations and the politics of coalition building favor at least a limited delay. The United States has reason to wait until it has made more progress against Al Qaeda and needs at least three to six months to fully prepare a major U.S. expeditionary force.

More generally, the United States would clearly benefit from better coalition building, which involves firmly persuading potential allies that the United States (1) has a clear plan to act quickly and decisively, (2) will commit all necessary force, and (3) has a post-Saddam plan for rebuilding a unified Iraq that will be desirable both to the Iraqi people and to Iraq's neighbors. It would also benefit from placing more emphasis on dialog with Iran than trying to match the posturing rhetoric of Iran's hardliners and from any step that can be taken to end the tragedy and ease the political backlash from the Second Intifada.

At the same time, the strategic situation does not favor indefinite delay. Prolonged containment might possibly allow the Gulf states, Iran, Turkey, and the West to ride out Saddam Hussein's regime without future conflicts. Unfortunately, containment may falter. It seems doubtful that sanctions on Iraqi arms imports can be sustained forever, and Iraq is virtually certain to perfect biological weapons with nuclear lethalities even if it cannot obtain nuclear weapons. Difficult and uncertain as a major military operation may seem today, the difficulties are likely to grow steadily with time. So is the threat that Saddam Hussein's Iraq can pose to the region.

U.S. Forces and Allied Capabilities

There are immense disparities between U.S. and Iraqi military forces and in the support the United States and Iraq may receive from other states. Although the United States cannot begin to bring all of its military capabilities to bear in an area halfway around the world, it does have a vast pool of forces to draw upon. The United States cannot at this point count on publicly declared support and contributions from its allies inside or outside the Gulf, but it is certain to have such support from a number of countries at the time it begins an invasion. Put differently, the United States will have support from an unpredictable mix of allies that will be of great strategic value. Saddam Hussein's regime can only count on sympathetic but largely insincere political rhetoric.

The Total Pool of U.S. Forces

As of April 2002, the United States had a total pool of roughly 1.4 million active forces in uniform, 1.28 million active and standby reserves, and some 667,000 civilian employees—many who perform functions performed by the military in Iraq. The war in Afghanistan has led to major changes in the normal deployments of U.S. forces, The U.S. Army had 481,300 men, and the U.S. Navy (USN) had 381,900. The U.S. Marine Corps (USMC) had 172,700, and the U.S. Air Force (USAF) had 362,300.[28] U.S. Special Forces included some 15,000 men in the U.S. Army, 4,000 in the U.S. Navy, and 9,320 in the U.S. Air Force.

The total strength of U.S. combat forces is constantly evolving, but the latest figures the Department of Defense reports in its *Defense Almanac* provide a reasonable approximation of U.S. capabilities. U.S. land forces included 10 active and 8 U.S. Army reserve divisions and 3 active and 1 reserve U.S. Army divisions, plus 3 active and 18 reserve U.S. Army brigades. The army had some 7,000 main battle tanks, 7,000 major other armored vehicles, 6,000 artillery weapons, and 1,500 armed helicopters. The U.S. Marine Corps had 3 active and 1 reserve divisions, with some 400 main battle tanks, 1,700 light armored and combat vehicles, 330 artillery weapons, and 190 armed helicopters.

U.S. conventional air forces included 46 USAF squadrons with 906 active attack and fighter aircraft, plus 38 squadrons and 549 combat aircraft in the reserves. It has some 16 B-2s and 56 additional B-52s it can use for conventional missions in its strategic forces. There were also a total of 82 B-1 bombers with 36 active and 16 reserve B-1B bombers in conventional roles. U.S. forces included 36 USN squadrons with 432 active attack and fighter aircraft, plus 3 squadrons and 36 combat

---

28. These figures are taken from the online edition of the U.S. Department of Defense's *Defense Almanac*, http://www.defenselink.mil/pubs/almanac/, accessed as of July 21, 2002.

aircraft in the reserves, and 21 USMC squadrons with 280 active attack and fighter aircraft, plus 4 squadrons and 48 combat aircraft in the reserves.

The U.S. Navy has shrunk nearly 40 percent since the Gulf War. Nevertheless, it had 259 combat ships in its battle forces, plus 18 SSBNS, 25 support ships, and 15 reserve ships, for a total battle force of 317 ships. These included 12 aircraft carriers and extensive amphibious, mine warfare, and cruise missile launch-capable ships.

Although any discussion of "normal" deployments has become moot since September 2001, roughly 1.1 million military are permanently deployed in the United States, 117,000 in Europe, 160 in the former Soviet Union, and 101,000 in Asia. Another 220 are deployed in sub-Saharan Africa, and 5,400 elsewhere in the Western Hemisphere. (These figures include afloat personnel.)

The totals permanently assigned to the Middle East, North Africa, Central Asia, and South Asia are changing so rapidly that any estimates are hopelessly dated. However, the most recent figures are 29,384 for the entire region, of which 14,772 were afloat in the Red Sea, Gulf, and Indian Ocean. The permanently stationed personnel in countries that would directly affect a contingency involving Iraq included 949 in Bahrain, 625 in Diego Garcia, 499 in Egypt, 36 in Israel, 29 in Jordan, 4,602 in Kuwait, 251 in Oman, 22 in Pakistan, 52 in Qatar, 7,053 in Saudi Arabia, 9 in Syria, 402 in the United Arab Emirates, and 4 in Yemen. These figures are so dated, however, that they do not reflect the fact that the United States has slowly cut its presence in the Kingdom in recent years. For example, in September 2001, the United States had some 650 army personnel manning a Patriot and signals unit on six-month rotations, some 4,800 men in rotational units that were enforcing the southern no-fly zone, 20 USN personnel, and 250 USMC personnel.

Uncertain Role of Allied and Neighboring States

No one can predict how much support the United States will get in creating a coalition to overthrow Saddam. It is almost a tautology, however, that the United States will not deploy forces for a major invasion unless it gets a critical pool of allies in the region that are willing to provide the support it needs. It is a fact that at this point in time, no nation in the region has expressed support of a major U.S. military operation, and even Kuwait has said that it would only support such action if directly authorized by the UN, and the only Western government whose leader has indicated that it would support the United States is Britain. At the same time, nations often change their minds when they come under direct pressure from the United States and the president presents specific plans and options. It is also a fact that Iraq would face threats in terms of the attitudes and military behavior of some of its neighbors even if they did not openly or fully support the United States.

Britain can make a major contribution to a U.S.-led coalition. Like U.S. forces, British forces are far smaller than at the time of the Gulf War. Britain could, however, still deploy an expeditionary force of at least two brigades, extensive air and naval forces, and excellent Special Forces. Its forces also offer the highest level of interoperability with U.S. forces. They would be primarily lift, sustainment/logistic, and base-limited, but UK's forces include some 212,000 men in uniform. Its army has some 114,000 men with extensive armored, mechanized, heliborne, and Special Forces elements; it includes a total of 616 main battle tanks, well over 2,500 other armored vehicles, and more than 450 artillery weapons. At least one two-brigade division in this force—the 1(UK) Armored Division—seems to be undergoing training and organization for this kind of expeditionary operation.[29] As a result, Britain might be able to deploy a force of some 25,000 men for such a contingency.

The RAF has roughly 50,000 men and some 430 combat aircraft. The Royal Navy has 16 submarines and 34 principal combatants. It can deploy up to two light carrier task forces, with roughly 20 combat aircraft and helicopters each, plus 21 mine countermeasure ships, patrol boats, and six amphibious ships. The UK normally deploys a small Armilla Patrol in the Gulf and Indian Ocean, with two combat ships and a small team of fewer than 50 men in Oman.[30]

France has severely underfunded its power projection capabilities and has never properly supported the plans of its military with the resources they need. It does, however, have the ability to stage and support brigade-sized Foreign Legion and heliborne forces in the Gulf. France normally stations some 4,200 men in the Indian Ocean area and 3,200 in Djibouti. These include an Indian Ocean squadron with two marine regiments and approximately 2,800 light mechanized forces with helicopters, plus a small number of combat aircraft. France could deploy one light carrier task force with 25 combat aircraft or a larger number of combat helicopters. It has extensive land-based combat air assets, and the UAE and Qatar operate French aircraft and could provide some logistic and maintenance support. A wide range of other NATO powers could provide limited contributions of specialized combat forces, help in securing Iraq for nation-building purposes, and offer basing, staging, and logistic support.

Although no neighbor of Iraq has yet expressed a willingness to commit military forces against Iraq—and their willingness to do so at the point a U.S.-led invasion becomes a reality is currently a matter of speculation—several have at least discussed such cooperation.

Turkey, for example, is a critical potential ally and has been the subject of several high-level visits since the Bush administration came to office. These discussions have involved incentives like aid, debt forgiveness, a public U.S. guarantee that there would be no Kurdish state, guarantees that the Turkish economy would not suffer from another war, and pledges that the United States would support an effective nation-building effort.[31]

The United States is more likely to ask Turkey for basing and staging facilities than military forces, but Turkey is a major military power. As already mentioned, it has repeatedly intervened in strength in northern Iraq in recent years (up to 30,000 men). It has a total of 609,000 men in uniform and nine army corps with a total of 495,000 men in its army, more than 4,200 tanks, roughly 4,000 other armored vehicles, and more than 2,800 artillery weapons. Its air force has some 60,000 men and more than 500 combat aircraft. Its navy has some 54,000 men, 14 submarines, 22

---

29. *Daily Telegraph* (London), July 19, 2002, p. 1.

30. These estimates are based largely on data in the IISS, *Military Balance, 2001–2002*.

31. *Dallas Morning News*, July 18, 2002; *Washington Post*, July 18, 2002, p. 26; *Los Angeles Times*, July 17, 2002; *Washington Post*, July 17, 2002, p. 18; *Wall Street Journal*, July 19, 2002.

major combat ships, 21 missile craft, 28 patrol craft, and 24 minelayers, but the Turkish navy is not organized to project power into the Gulf region.

The southern Gulf states have many military weaknesses and so far have shown little willingness to provide forces for military action against Iraq. They do, however, have major basing and logistic assets. Oman has long provided pre-positioning and air basing. The UAE has provided port facilities and has agreed to pre-position a U.S. Army brigade set. Bahrain, Kuwait, and Qatar have long provided air basing and are steadily improving their facilities. Kuwait and Qatar already pre-position the heavy combat equipment for one U.S. Army brigade set each and substantial amounts of other equipment and munitions. Bahrain hosts the U.S. fleet in the Gulf, and Kuwait can serve as a major staging area for U.S. ground troops operating against Iraq. Kuwait would also almost certainly deploy all four of its brigades, its Patriots, and its air force to defend its borders, which would help secure the flanks and rear areas of U.S. and British forces.

Saudi Arabia can provide excellent ports and air bases and strategic depth for both air and land operations against Iraq. Its willingness to do so in the face of its problems with Islamist extremists and the popular backlash against the Second Intifada is more speculative than that of the other Gulf states, but Saudi cooperation could take many forms. Saudi Arabia has already provided command and control, airspace access, and some staging facilities for the U.S. operation in Afghanistan. Even if its forces never cross the Iraqi border, they provide air defense on a critical border and may well force Iraq to disperse forces to defend against the very possibility of an attack from the west. "Passive" Saudi support in terms of access to airspace, C^4I facilities, and recovery bases for air operations could be of great value, although the United States has now duplicated its critical Saudi C^4I facilities in other Gulf states, and these are less critical than in the past. The fact that Saudi land and air forces would have to deploy to guard the Saudi border would help secure the flanks and rear areas of any U.S. operations in Kuwait, and Saudi Arabia might quietly allow U.S. aircraft based in the kingdom to fly "defensive" air-combat and SEAD missions. More extensive support in terms of water, POL, port facilities, and air bases would be of similar value, and Saudi willingness to allow U.S. ground troops to operate from Saudi Arabia would confront Iraq with having to disperse its heavy divisions in ways that would seriously strain its logistic, mobility, and command capabilities even if these Iraqi forces remained concentrated in central Iraq.

Although Iraq may see Jordan primarily as a tool in its struggle to exploit the Second Intifada and win acceptance in the Arab world, Jordan too is a potential threat to Iraq. Iraq has to face the reality that Jordan probably would not resist Israeli use of its air space. It cannot totally dismiss the possibility that the United States might obtain access to air bases and even be able to move in land and combat helicopter forces for some kind of attack from the west. Bases like the Muafaq Al-Salti Air Base, Al Azraq Air Base, and Al Jafr Air Base support Jordanian F-16s, or have U.S. compatible equipment, and would be particularly good staging points.[32] King Abdullah faces strong popular opposition to any support of the United States,

---

32. Washingtonpost.com, July 15, 2002.

but a more stable, friendly Iraq free of sanctions could be of immense strategic and economic benefit to Jordan, and Jordan's government can have no illusions about the sincerity of Iraqi "friendship."

Iran also presents a problem for Iraq regardless of how hostile Iran may be to a U.S. military action. Iran may not be strong enough to challenge Iraq by itself, but the fact remains that Iraq faces the constant risk that Iran may exploit any U.S. defeat of Iraq. Ironically, this risk is greatest in terms of a covert operation, opposition overthrow, or limited U.S. military involvement in Iraq, since it is in these contingencies that Iran could do most to try to exploit Shi'ite unrest and the Iranian-based Iraqi opposition. Iraq learned during the Gulf War that even seeming Iranian support could quickly turn into the confiscation of a large part of the Iraqi air force. It must be careful in drawing down upon its ground forces to deal with a U.S.-led attack. Iran also is not strong enough militarily to act on the hostility of its hard-liners to the United States. It must tolerate U.S. military action even if it opposes it politically, and "axis of evil" aside, the Khatami faction of the Iranian government and Iranian people are well aware that the Bush administration's hostility only applies to one element of a deeply divided Iranian government.

A U.S. invasion of Iraq may well frighten Iranian hard-liners with the prospect of U.S. encirclement, but they are scarcely in a military position to challenge the military capabilities of the United States. U.S. assurances and informal dialog might well, on the other hand reassure Khatami, more moderate Iranian political leaders, and the Iranian people. Getting rid of a hostile and aggressive Iraq would greatly ease Iran's security problems and reduce its near- and long-term incentive to proliferate. A clear U.S. commitment to ensuring the rights of Iraqi Shi'ites and to a form of nation building that offered both the hope of Iraqi stability and the certainty of U.S. withdrawal would also ease tensions with Iran.

Although Israel is generally perceived as an American strategic liability because its involvement might weaken the support Arab allies provide to the United States, Iraq also faces the risk that any military adventures against Israel could at a minimum lead to major new air strikes on Iraq that would probably show far less concern over collateral damage than U.S. military action and at most devastate Iraq as a nation. Saddam Hussein's willingness to commit suicide in a last gesture or take massive military risks in the hope Arab governments would turn against a U.S. military operation in mid-conflict may or may not be exaggerated. The practical military consequences of any such Israeli adventure to Iraq, however, may well be far more serious than the level of strategic annoyance they cause the United States.

Current U.S. Capabilities in the Gulf

Land Warfare

For all its global military strength, the United States is scarcely organized for an immediate war with Iraq, and any estimates of the U.S. forces currently in the region do not reflect the U.S. power projection capabilities that would be deployed in an Iraqi contingency. In June 2002, however, the United States had a total force of 55,000 military personnel from all services in the entire theater. Many were assigned to the Afghan conflict, with 7,500 in Afghanistan, 1,000 in Pakistan, 1,000 in Kyrgyzstan, 1,700 in Uzbekistan, and 13,000 afloat. In addition, the United States had 5,100 personnel in Saudi Arabia, 3,900 in Qatar, 3,500 in Oman, 4,500 in Bahrain, 850 in the UAE, and 64 in Yemen. (The Gulf numbers had dropped since April 2002 because of movements into the theater and because of cuts in the naval presence that dropped the personnel afloat by 9,000.) The United States had a total of 570 aircraft for the entire CENTCOM area, including the Afghan conflict, which included 195 fixed-wing shooters, 40 attack helicopters, 125 support helicopters, 110 fixed-wing cargo aircraft, 40 ISR aircraft, 60 tankers, and 90 allied coalition aircraft.[33]

It should be noted that many senior U.S. commanders would strongly prefer to continue devoting such assets to the attack on Al Qaeda through early or mid-2003. They in no way oppose U.S. operations against Iraq, but would like to make substantial further progress in the war on terrorism before conducting a major operation against Saddam Hussein's regime.

The United States did not have any major land combat units forward deployed into the Gulf in mid-2002, although it had some combat elements in Kuwait. The U.S. Army stocked equipment for three heavy brigades in the Gulf area. Two brigade sets were pre-positioned in Kuwait, and the other set (which includes equipment to support a division headquarters) was located in Qatar. Another brigade set was pre-positioned at sea. Pre-positioning of a fifth set is planned for the UAE but probably will not be completed before such a contingency takes place. The U.S. Air Force stores air-base operation sets in several southern Gulf countries, many of which are being used to support contingency operations.

In the past, pre-positioned U.S. land and air forces did not have all of the equipment necessary to fully deploy as combat forces. U.S. Army brigade sets used older major combat equipment and did not have all of their combat support and logistic equipment. They did not have all of the other combat and service-support equipment needed, and they lacked the ability to provide water and POL to maneuver forces. There are indicators, however, that the United States (and possibly Britain) has begun quietly deploying all of these elements into Qatar, Bahrain, and Kuwait and forward deploying munitions and supplies into the areas where they would base combat operations. Maritime movement and pre-positioning capabilities may also have been changed, possibly including added pre-positioning of air munitions and supplies to Turkey. Since the movement and preparation of equipment and sustainment is the key factor that delays a buildup, the United States (and possibly Britain) may be able to deploy against Iraq far more quickly than is generally recognized.

The United States can draw on a broader pool of pre-positioning ships both at Diego Garcia and in the Pacific. It uses a mix of government-owned ships and commercial vessels to stockpile materiel at sea. Army equipment and supplies are carried aboard a fleet of chartered vessels, LMSRs, and a Ready Reserve Force (RRF) ship. These forces are stationed in the Indian and Pacific Oceans and provide materiel for an armor brigade and selected combat support and combat service support units.

---

33. U.S. Department of Defense, Public Affairs Office, June 27, 2002.

Additionally, the fleet carries army watercraft for port-opening operations. Plans call for an additional army brigade set to be pre-positioned afloat in the near term.

Marine Corps equipment and supplies are carried on 14 vessels operating with the Maritime Pre-positioning Force (MPF). The ships are organized into three squadrons, each capable of supporting a 17,300-person Marine Expeditionary Brigade (MEB) for 30 days. The squadrons are stationed in the western Pacific, Indian Ocean, and Mediterranean Sea. Plans call for two new vessels to be added to the MPF in the near term. These ships, converted specifically for MPF operations, will be allocated between two MPF squadrons. The U.S. sea-based pre-positioning force also includes three chartered ships carrying air force munitions. Additionally, there is an RRF tanker and two RRF ships specially equipped to transfer fuel directly ashore.

Pre-positioning ships at Diego Garcia had the equivalent of another brigade set—plus substantial support equipment and supplies—but normally required 11–17 days to make ready and move. The United States did, however, have substantial supplies and basing facilities in Bahrain, Qatar, the UAE, and Oman plus the air units in forces enforcing the southern no-fly zone in Saudi Arabia.

The United States can draw upon a pool of five light and heavy divisions for relatively quick expeditionary operations. These forces normally require months of specialized training, preparation, and reorganization for sustained operations against heavy enemy forces with extensive armor and artillery, although the U.S. Army may have begun to quietly carry out such actions. These units are also significantly less combat capable than in 1991, because the army has eliminated some 25 percent of the combat battalions in such units, while keeping all of the headquarters and command slots.

For all of the talk of a revolution in military affairs and an "army of the future," U.S. Army experts differ over just how far the U.S. Army has advanced in several mission-critical areas:

- Reliance on past concepts of force density and required numbers to achieve overwhelming force

- The ability to mix elements of light and heavy forces rather than rigidly rely on the formation and unit structure of the present combat forces

- Willingness to risk relying on less heavy combat systems like artillery and measures to lighten logistic and lift requirements

- Willingness to rely on airpower to secure the flanks of major offensive thrusts rather than advance as broad offensives

- Willingness to risk deploying follow-on forces after the air and land campaign begin rather than deploy all forces to the theater before land combat begins

- Willingness to aggressively commit attack helicopter and heliborne forces to unsecured forward bases and locations or rely on airpower to secure their facilities

- Willingness and ability to make the most effective use of close air support coupled to a USAF emphasis on interdiction and rear area bombing

- Ability to handle the bridging requirements necessary to cross water barriers like the Euphrates

■ Arrangements to effectively mix U.S. Army, USN, and USMC special force equivalents and make use of ships and other non-army platforms to base such operations

■ Real-world capability to handle the civil-military aspects of occupying Iraq and
aid the Iraqi regime that replaces Saddam Hussein in nation building.

The U.S. Marine Corps could deploy one light division-sized MEF, with both
land and air elements, by sea in a number of weeks and two within 30 days. U.S.
Marine Corps units are notably better organized and trained for expeditionary
operations than the U.S. Army, but have limited armored and artillery strength and
limited combat support, service support, and sustainability away from amphibious
and support ships.

U.S. air and missile power can be deployed much more rapidly than U.S. land
power. Limits on the buildup of U.S. air forces would be set by the availability of
basing, airspace access, and munitions stocks and by the availability of more scarce
assets like intelligence, aircraft control and warning (AC&W), and ISR aircraft.

The availability of ports, staging areas, water, and petroleum, oil, and lubricants
(POL) would all be key factors affecting the size of the U.S. ground forces that could
be deployed and might be so capacity-limited that the United States could only
involve outside ground forces in a U.S.-led coalition at the expense of cutting its
own land force deployments. The availability of Kuwaiti, Saudi, Turkish, and/or
Jordanian "ground space" would be critical in determining the size of any Western
ground force that could be sustained in the region as well as the number of axis of
attack, flexibility of maneuver, and logistic support requirements. In broad terms,
the U.S. Army would need more and more specialized training and specialized reorganization in proportion to the limits to the "ground space" available and would
become more dependent on air and missile power both to prepare the battlefield
and provide ongoing support during combat operations.

Allied support could reduce the amount of ground forces the United States
would have to contribute and the time needed for preparation and deployment, but
would involve trade-offs. Britain could contribute and sustain a force of several brigades, but this would force it to draw down on virtually all of its deployable assets,
equipment reserves, munitions reserves, and transportation and lift capabilities. No
other European force could deploy and sustain heavy brigades in the Gulf without
imposing a disruptive burden on U.S. logistic and lift assets—even if the political
decision was taken to commit such forces. France could, however, deploy at least
one light regiment with significant attack helicopters and heliborne lift. (The problems French forces encountered during the Gulf War were at least partly due to the
stalling tactics of the French minister of defense at the time, who failed to commit
the assets requested by the French military.) Many other countries could contribute
specialized units to compensate for shortfalls in the U.S. Army and USMC, but significant training and some changes in communications equipment would be
necessary to make them interoperable.

The land forces of the southern Gulf states offer the potential advantage that
they would not compete with U.S. ground forces for limited port, basing, and logistic facilities, and have exercised with U.S. forces in the past. No regional Arab ground
force is effective enough, however, to play a major role in leading an offensive against

Iraqi main force divisions, but Arab land forces could help secure the flanks of a U.S. offensive, provide rear area security, and perform peacekeeping functions. Kuwaiti involvement could present serious problems in terms of future regional tensions unless it could be managed as part of a broad effort to liberate Iraq that was followed by a form of nation building that clearly aided the Iraqi people and involved steps like forgiveness of debt and reparations. The same is true to a lesser extent of Saudi and Jordanian forces. In general, an Arab military role in liberating and rebuilding Iraq might offer both the United States and the region a much better strategic outcome than direct Arab participation in offensive ground operations.

The Turkish army is a very different story in military terms. Once again ignoring political factors—Turkish domestic and Iraqi Kurdish and Arab fears of the Turks—Turkey could mount a corps-size land operation against northern Iraq in fewer than 30 days. If such an offensive had extensive U.S. and Turkish air support, the Iraqi army would not be capable of effective forward defense.

Air and Missile Warfare

The size of the air forces the USAF, USN, and USMC could contribute is likely to be base, lift, and support-limited rather than force-limited. It would also be sharply affected by the level of precision munitions available and U.S. ability to concentrate what are often relatively limited intelligence and strategic reconnaissance, airborne command and control, other expeditionary C^4I/battle management assets to support one major regional contingency in spite of the operation against Al Qaeda, and the risks posed by threats like North Korea. The United States is constantly changing its expeditionary force mix to substitute precision munitions, improved targeting, and more rapid command decisions for platform numbers. Table 6.1, however, provides a picture of the assets the United States has used in other recent conflicts.

The United States could certainly rapidly deploy the equivalent of 5–7 air wings if basing, POL, water, and pre-positioned munitions and critical spares were available and could rapidly build up additional forces. In practice, however, the United States is strategic airlift–limited, and its land and air forces must compete for strategic airlift assets. Basing is also critical. The U.S., British, and allied air forces saturated all surplus basing capability in the southern Gulf during the Gulf War, and the United States made use of Diego Garcia. This involved a total of some 23 air bases, and 11 of these—and by far the best—were in Saudi Arabia.

Major improvements have taken place in the air bases in Bahrain, Kuwait, and Qatar since the time of the Gulf War, but the United States and its allies would still be seriously base-limited if Saudi Arabia did not make its bases available. Access to Saudi air space would also be critical for overflights, staging offensive air formations, refueling operations, and attacking from a wide range of vectors. Access to Turkish bases and air space would be equally critical.

The United States would face other limits. Any critical shortfall in precision munitions is likely to be corrected by the time the United States is ready to conduct a massive air operation in support of a ground offensive. As has been mentioned earlier, the day-to-day availability of strategic airlift would be important, but so would U.S. ability to concentrate most of its global assets of tanker, AC&W, ISR, air

Table 6.1. U.S. Airpower in Recent Regional Conflicts

	Desert Storm	Serbia/Kosovo	Afghanistan
Area of operations (sq. miles)	176,000	39,500	250,000
Length of war (days)	43	78	?
Total sorties during period reported	118,700	37,500–38,000	29,000–38,000*
Percentage of total U.S. sorties flown*	85	60	92
Offensive strike sorties	41,300	10,808–14,006**	17,500
Sorties per day	2,800	200, climbing to 2,000	25, climbing to 200
Total bombs delivered*	265,000	23,000	22,000
Precision-guided bombs delivered*	20,450	8,050	12,500
Percentage of total munitions that are precision-guided	7–8%	35%	56%
Percentage of U.S. precision-guided weapons delivered	89	80	99
Combat losses	38	2	0

*Data based on Michael E. O'Hanlon and an estimate of 38,000 sorties flown.

**The USAF reported a normal figure of 12,600 "shooter sorties." See Anthony H. Cordesman, *The Lessons and Non-Lessons of the Air and Missile Campaign in Kosovo* (Westport: Praeger, 2001), 42–44.

Note: Significant definitional problems exist in making such counts, and historical sources differ. This count is based on the work of Thomas Keaney at Johns Hopkins University and on Michael E. O'Hanlon, "A Flawed Masterpiece," *Foreign Affairs* 81, no. 3 (March/April 2002): 52. O'Hanlon evidently reports on a longer period than Keaney.

defense suppression, ground-based air expeditionary, and other specialized elements in support of the air campaign against Iraq—at least during the initial weeks of the campaign. This would create potential vulnerabilities in areas like Korea and the Taiwan strait and could present problems for the operation against Al Qaeda. These same factors would limit U.S. capability to support allied air forces. Moreover, only the air forces of Britain, France, Kuwait, Saudi Arabia, and Turkey would have significant *initial* interoperability with U.S. air units in the kind of missions involved.

U.S. carriers could substitute for land-based operations to some extent, although intensive long-endurance carrier-based missions require support from land-based refueling, ISR, and AC&W assets and emergency rescue and landing capability. As a rough rule of thumb, a carrier can deploy 60 combat aircraft that are useful in this type of combat operations, and three carriers are needed to support continuing operations 24 hours a day (two working and one in supporting, refitting, and restoring capability). The United States could deploy a force of six carriers to the region, although only four would probably deploy in the Gulf. The USN could, however, be support-ship-limited. It has made serious cuts in oilers and at-sea replenishment capability since the Gulf War. European carriers—even if available—have a much smaller aircraft load, have far less sophisticated combat aircraft, mission payload capability, precision weapon delivery capability, and sortie rate generation and sustainment capability.

As is the case with U.S. ground forces, the use of U.S. air and missile power also raises questions about the role service biases and military bureaucracy could play in spite of the so-called revolution in military affairs. U.S. air and naval experts differ over just how far the U.S. Army has advanced in several critical areas:

- Ability to sharply reduce the decision time and speed the targeting-strike-restrike cycle

- Effective integration of all ISR assets and ability to reshape the mix of ISR assets to handle the specific mission requirements in Iraq, including targeting and damage assessment in urban, built-up, and other civilian areas

- Continuing problems in orienting National Technical Means (NTM), electronic intelligence (ELINT), and signals intelligence (SIGINT) to effectively support theater military operations rather than "inform" policymakers in Washington

- Willingness to face the real-world failure of past "strategic" strikes on leadership, logistic, infrastructure, communications, and POL targets to achieve anything like the results initially claimed in the Gulf War and Kosovo; willingness to focus on decisive land/air operations against critical objectives like Baghdad versus "bomb an entire country"

- Surviving USAF bias against true jointness in the form of emphasizing close air support, military-target-oriented interdiction operations, and integration of fixed and rotary wing-operations

- Ability to honestly assess the severe remaining problems in targeting and battle damage assessment

- Military problems in accurately assessing the ability of air and missile power to target critical dispersed infantry and land weapons targets and realistically assess damage; process in dealing with decoys and deception

- Civil-military problems in developing effective rules of engagement and procedures to deal with the problem of civilian casualties and collateral damage

- Ability to use airpower to support land forces in operating across water barriers like the Euphrates

- Willingness to take casualties to operate directly over Iraqi urban areas with heavy land-based air defenses, impact of shortfalls in electronic warfare aircraft, and problems with current anti-radiation missiles and other suppression of enemy air defense (SEAD) assets

■ Level of explicit planning to deal with the range of possible Iraqi uses of missiles and CBRN weapons

■ Real-world capability to handle the civil-military aspects of occupying Iraq and aid the Iraqi regime that replaces Saddam Hussein in nation building.

The United States has, however, made major advances in sea- and air-launched cruise missile capability and related precision-targeting capability since the Gulf War. These advances give U.S. and British cruise missile ships and aircraft a highly reliable cruise missile strike capability and the replacement of TERCOM with GPS guidance provides 10-meter operational accuracy and allows the missile flight path to be varied in each attack—avoiding the Gulf War pattern of flying follow-on strikes down predictable corridors because of terrain mapping needs.

U.S. B-52, B-1B, and B-2 bombers could operate from the United States and Diego Garcia. All can now deliver large amounts of precision munitions per sortie. The B-2 has extensive stealth capabilities, as does the stealth strike fighter. All could deliver precision munitions from strike points deep in Iraq, and could penetrate even within range of Iraqi cities and strong points once (and if) the United States suppressed Iraqi ground-based air defenses.

Finally, Iraq has some 20–40 airfields that could be seized and occupied to create new U.S. air bases for the combat aircraft in a U.S.-led coalition, as well as used by attack helicopters, troop helicopters, and airlift. Many are in comparatively remote areas from Iraqi cities, air defense, and normal ground force deployments. Special Forces and light ground forces could flow in through such bases, and U.S. Patriot units could provide forward and rear area air and missile defenses.

Land forces can also support key air warfare missions. Advancing ground troops, Special Forces, and ranger-like units can attack Iraqi ground-based air defenses, attack Iraqi command-and-control facilities and communications nets, and CBRN facilities. They also can now make far better use of intelligence and communications to provide GPS data and laser illumination for target air and cruise missile strikes.

Covert Overthrow

The simplest such U.S. attack that Iraq would have to deal with would avoid any of these basing and commitment limitations on U.S. and allied forces. It would be a covert overthrow effort, focusing on the use of outside opposition and covert efforts to support internal opposition, possibly mixed with attacks directly on the leadership of the regime by U.S. agents or their proxies (a decapitation scenario). Iraq already seems to face such a threat. *USA Today* and the *Washington Post* have both reported that President Bush signed a Presidential Finding in February 2002 that called for (1) increased support to the opposition, including providing weapons and training; (2) expanded intelligence collection efforts within Iraq linked to both encouraging Saddam Hussein's overthrow, and gathering information and targeting data on the leadership, key military facilities, and key CBRN facilities, and (3) possible use of CIA and Special Forces teams to operate in Iraq that could kill

Saddam and his leadership coterie in "self defense."[34] The United States and Britain also seem to have made significant increases in their intelligence collection efforts in Iraq, both for overthrow and targeting purposes.[35]

Iraq's security services are well organized to deal with such contingencies and have shown in the past that they can thoroughly penetrate opposition groups inside and outside Iraq. They have dealt with many past coup attempts and plots, and the odds of U.S. success must be seen as limited unless the regime weakens seriously for internal reasons that currently cannot be predicted.

Amatzia Baram has analyzed this aspect of Iraqi security forces in some detail.[36] He reports that Saddam's immediate bodyguard is drawn from members of Saddam's al-Bu Nasir tribe, most of whom come from the area around his birthplace in Tikrit and Ujah—the village he grew up in. Many commanders in both the military and security forces also come from these towns, although the al-Bu Nasir tribe only has around 25,000—30,0000 members, Tikrit only about 40,000 inhabitants, and Ujah about 10,000. He also estimates, however, that the total number of Sunnis in affiliated tribes and regions makes up 15–17 percent of the roughly 19 million that he calculates are still under the regime's direct control.

The main security detachment that immediately surrounds the president is the Presidential Protection Force (Himaya or Himayat al Ra'is), which has several thousand men from Saddam's tribe and is responsible for protecting the presidential palaces, Saddam's various dispersed residences, and the houses of some other members of Saddam's elite. This force is recruited while young men are still 15–16 years old, and they are kept in training in the palace areas for three years in order to indoctrinate them and ensure their loyalty. They have a 40-man inner bodyguard called the Murafiqin. Its top commanders hold the rank of foremost companion (Murafiq Aqdam) and general, and the group is recruited from the al-Beigat, Saddam's subsection of the al-Bu Nasir tribe.

Saddam depends heavily on the Special Security Organization (SSO or Al-Amn al-Khass), a security organization with several thousand members—many of whom are officers and come from Tikrit or are members of the al-Bu Nasir. This force is under the command of Saddam's younger son Qusay and Saddam's personal secretary, General Abd Ihmid Hmud. In addition to acting on its own with decisive brutality, the SSO coordinates the activities of the other security agencies and has been ruthless in removing suspects from within them. It controls the political prisons at Radwaniya and Abu Gharib.[37]

In addition to the military intelligence and various Republican Guards forces discussed earlier, there are several thousand men in the General Intelligence Directorate (GID or Da'irat Al Mukhabarat al-Amma). Although intelligence is the main function of the GID, it also has strong counterintelligence elements. According to Amatzia Baram, it has been strong enough to challenge Saddam's oldest son, Udayy,

---

34. *USA Today* first reported this on February 28, 2002; the *Washington Post* reported it on June 16, 2002. More uncertain reports that the UK is also using agents in Iraq to incite revolts have been published in the *Daily Telegraph* (July 12, 2002, p. 1).

35. *Washington Times*, July 17, 2002, p. 11.

36. Baram, "The Iraqi Armed Forces and Security Apparatus," pp. 113–123.

37. Ibid.

over his smuggling operations. Udayy too, however, has his own security force—the Feda'iyyi-Saddam—with some 10,000 young men who act in a police capacity, but also perform security tasks.[38]

Saddam, who has a long history of moving unexpectedly from site to site, has more than 15 presidential compounds, or palaces, and a number of underground shelters. He uses doubles and complex convoys for road movement, and those with access to him are subject to extensive search. He surrounds himself with small, trusted coteries—including his sons, General Hmud (head of the SSO), Vice President Taha Yasin Ramadan, Deputy Prime Minister Tariq Aziz, and Izzat Ibrahim, the deputy chairman of the Revolutionary Command Council. He regularly rotates the commanders and officials in positions who could threaten him, and Tikritis and Nasiris also staff many sensitive middle- and lower-ranking positions.

This pervasive security structure is the product of nearly three decades of experience with coup and assassination attempts. It has protected Saddam on many occasions, and the war in Afghanistan has shown that it is far easier to talk about attacking leaders than actually find them.

At the same time, the Iraqi regime is scarcely immune to family and tribal feuds and conflicts over power, prestige, and money. The fact that so many are excluded from the elite, and the ruthlessness and brutality with which internal security operations are conducted, creates fault lines and possible vulnerabilities. So does the fact that Saddam and others in the elite around him only have to make one critical mistake in terms of allowing the United States to target and attack them. Intelligence and targeting are never consistently perfect, but they can sporadically be truly excellent.

At a minimum, a U.S. overthrow effort puts constant pressure on the Iraqi regime. Like the no-fly zones, it reinforces containment, increases the credibility of any future UN inspection effort, and would aid in targeting U.S. air and missile strikes if the United States escalates to the open use of military force. The political backlash is limited by the fact that the United States will be accused of such action whether or not it takes it, and such efforts scarcely violate regional practices and norms. Certainly, the death of Saddam Hussein and those around him would be celebrated by many and mourned only by the purist advocates of human rights and international law. The United States may also be more successful with a carefully targeted covert propaganda effort than it has been in its dismal overt diplomatic efforts.

At the same time, such a U.S. effort is likely to reinforce the Iraqi regime's conviction that it must plan for much higher levels of attack on the regime and that the use of CBRN weapons is necessary. It is also hard to argue that the United States can legitimately carry out covert operations and Iraq cannot. The fact the United States has such efforts under way tends to make plots against Saddam, and opposition groups with ties to the United States, appear as treason. Furthermore, any conspicuous failures, in terms of failed plots and U.S. effort, will be seen in Iraq and in the region as major victories and will be portrayed in exaggerated terms out of any proportion to the true cost of the United States.

---

38. Ibid.

Opposition Ground Forces and U.S. Airpower: "Afghan Option"

A second option, and one supported by some leading analysts and officials in the Bush administration, would be to deploy limited U.S. ground forces, rely largely on U.S. airpower, and use opposition ground forces—possibly stiffened by U.S. Special Forces and advisory teams—to try to defeat Saddam's regime. Variations on this contingency involve creating a U.S. military "sanctuary" for the opposition inside the Kurdish security zone, Kuwait or western Iraq, and/or relying heavily on defections of Iraqi military forces and commanders as a result of U.S. and Iraqi opposition covert action.

Use of Opposition Ground Forces

As has been discussed earlier, the depth of the real-world loyalty of the Iraq military and security forces is a key "intangible." In spite of Saddam's long history of detecting and suppressing coups, success in using carrots and sticks to enforce loyalty, and the weakness of the opposition, many other repressive regimes have suddenly failed to deal with internal threats in the past. No one can conclusively dismiss the idea that the Iraqi regime and its military forces might suddenly collapse if put under serious pressure. There also is at least the possibility that such a collapse could be speeded by some form of decapitating strike on the Iraqi leadership by U.S. Special Forces, airpower, and/or agents.

The only current opposition force with any real-world military capability is the Iranian-backed SAIRI, which the United States is not currently likely to support or wish to have involved. Although some of the other Iraqi opposition groups outside Iraq have made grossly exaggerated claims about their ability to train military forces and conduct some kind of military operation to liberate Iraq, these claims are little more than political posturing. There may, however, be enough volunteers to provide several light regimental equivalents. Training and equipping such forces would take time and could not produce forces that could challenge regular Iraqi forces in combat, but might form a core of opposition forces that would lead some regular Iraqi forces to defect.

There are a number of senior Iraqi military defectors out of a total of up to 1,500 ex-Iraqi military living abroad, and some may still have support from the military forces in Iraq. The Iraqi National Congress has attempted to organize these defectors and has had some success. It held a meeting of such officers in London in July 2002 and created a 15-man Military Council with ex-Brigadier-General Tawfik al-Yassiri as its spokesman. However, only about 50 out of the INC's 90 invitees showed up, and many remain separate and aloof. These include General Nizar al-Khazraji, a former army chief of staff, who is the one defector who can legitimately claim to have been a major hero in the Iran-Iraq War, but whose role in the attack on Halabja is uncertain.[39]

---

39. *Times* (London), July 15, 2002; *New York Times*, July 14, 2002, p. 10; *Washington Times*, July 15, 2002, p. 1; *Wall Street Journal*, July 15, 2002.

Although the lessons of the U.S. and British military experience in Afghanistan may not translate directly into war-fighting experience in Iraq or any other case, they do show that factors like political and military leadership, morale, adaptability, and other intangibles could again lead to a far more rapid Iraqi collapse than Iraq's force numbers and Saddam's past ability to survive coup attempts would indicate.

The size of Taliban and Al Qaeda forces in Afghanistan—and the past performance of Afghan forces in their struggle with the forces of the former Soviet Union—proved to be a poor measure of actual Taliban and Al Qaeda war-fighting capability and endurance. It was not possible to predict how long Serbian forces would hold out in Kosovo or to tie estimates of battle damage either to confirmed kills or to Serbian political behavior. Similarly, the force ratios at the start of the Gulf War gave a greatly exaggerated picture of Iraqi military strength. So did Iraq's performance in the final battles of the Iran-Iraq War.

One key uncertainty is the extent to which the United States would risk a major "decapitation" strike by CIA operatives, Special Forces, and/or air and missile strikes to kill or capture Saddam, his sons, and the other leaders of the regime, and how successful such a strike would be. Saddam Hussein's rule is highly centralized and personal. Aside from his sons and a handful of those closest to him, there is little to hold it together if he should be captured or killed, and the cohesion of military operations and the operations of the security forces would be very uncertain *if* a decapitation option could really be executed. (It is far easier to postulate success than to achieve it.)

Limits to the Afghan Lesson

At the same time, the success of any effort that relies on the opposition and defections to do the ground fighting and deal with the problem of nation building seems unlikely. The military capabilities of the opposition are negligible compared with those of the Afghan warlords opposing the Taliban, and an "Afghan option" that relies largely on opposition forces with a limited stiffening of U.S. Special Forces and limited amounts of strike airpower does not seem likely to succeed.

The collapse of the Taliban took place with fewer than 300 forward-deployed U.S. Special Forces and roughly 80 U.S. strike/attack sorties per day in support of the Northern Alliance. However, the defeat of an extremely weak opponent like the Taliban is very different from fighting a much stronger opponent like Saddam Hussein's Iraq. Iraq is a far better organized, stronger, and more popular tyranny. It is a power with both modern internal security services and 2,200 tanks and heavy armored forces capable of serious war fighting. It retains an active air force and, more important, has rebuilt much of its land-based air defense net and has large numbers of surface-to-air missiles, radars, underground command centers, and redundant optical fiber command and control communications. It has at least some chemical and biological weapons and probably some surviving Scuds and extended-range Scuds.

Iraq has considerable strategic depth, and it is much easier to talk about the regime's unpopularity than to know what the population will actually do. Iraq is a nation of roughly 437,000 square kilometers or twice the size of Idaho. Although it has a coastline of only 58 kilometers, it has long borders that the regime can use to obtain access to other states. The border with Turkey is 331 kilometers, 181 kilometers with Jordan, 242 kilometers with Kuwait, 814 kilometers with Saudi Arabia, and 605 kilometers with Syria.

The sheer size of Iraq's population would make it a problem for small opposition forces to take over the country as well as present problems for any larger invasion force and nation-building effort. For all of Iraq's claims about hardship and high death rates, its population—now more than 23 million people—is one of the fastest growing in the world. Well over 60 percent were born after Saddam took power and have known no other ruler; well over 30 percent have been born since the Gulf War.[40] The CIA estimates that more than 271,000 young Iraqi males reach military age each year and that Iraq can draw on a military manpower pool of more than 3 million.

Saddam Hussein's regime is vulnerable because it is based on a dictatorship led by a small, largely Sunni elite taken primarily from tribal groups in the area around Tikrit. In addition, Iraq has deep ethnic divisions (Arab, 75–80 percent; Kurdish, 15–20 percent; Turkoman, Assyrian, or other, 5 percent) and religious divisions (Muslim, 97 percent [Shi'a, 60–65 percent; Sunni, 32–37 percent]; Christian or other, 3 percent). In the past, however, many Iraqi Shi'ites have been loyal to the regime, and the size of the Shi'ite uprisings in the south in 1991 is often exaggerated. It is not clear how many Iraqi Shi'ites would see a U.S.-sponsored opposition as "liberation" versus an "invasion." Once again, such factors are intangibles that *might* greatly reduce the need for opposition forces, but there is no way to predict what will actually happen. Furthermore, Kurdish and Shi'ite religious forces might well be seen as traitors by at least part of the Iraqi population.

Some of the uncertainties inherent in military "intangibles" could also favor Iraq. For example, Iraqi nationalism—and hostility to the United States because of the Gulf War and U.S. sanctions—could harden Iraqi military and popular resolve and produce stiffer resistance than during the defense of Kuwait. Planning on the virtual collapse of the Iraqi regime is planning for a possibility and not a probability. To put this in context, the speed of the catalytic collapse of the Taliban and Al Qaeda was always *possible*, but it was never *probable* or *certain*.

How Much U.S. Airpower Is Enough?
The Iraqi SEAD Challenge

There are dangers in using limited amounts of U.S. air and missile power as well as in relying on opposition ground forces. The United States has shown again and again that it has outstanding military forces and can make effective use of modern technology, but skill and technology are not a substitute for sufficient force and effective tactics. Over-reliance on airpower, particularly limited amounts of airpower, can have serious consequences.

One key uncertainty would be how rapidly the United States could suppress Iraqi surface-based air defenses in the populated areas, the level of U.S. airpower that would have to go into the suppression of enemy air defense, or SEAD, mission, and the effectiveness and survivability of short and medium land-based air defenses

---

40. CIA, *World Factbook*, 2001, http://www.odci.gov/cia/publications/factbook/index.html.

in dealing with attack helicopters, other helicopters, and fixed-wing aircraft forced into relatively short-range engagements.

Much of the U.S. and allied success in Bosnia, Kosovo, and Afghanistan has depended on the almost immediate achievement of near-total air supremacy and the ability to engage enemy ground forces in ways where they could make only limited or no use of their armor or artillery against U.S. and allied forces—aside from local allies and proxies.

The United States has shown that stealth, long-range stand-off munitions and the use of UAVs and unmanned aerial combat vehicles (UACVs) offer ways to greatly improve some aspects of SEAD capability and to target and attack even when extensive land-based air defenses are present. Nevertheless, SEAD remains a challenge in dealing a well-equipped and relatively sophisticated opponent like Iraq, and much still depends on the sophistication of the opponent's air and air defense assets, as well as the skill and determination with which they are used.

The problem would be particularly critical in the case of Baghdad and Iraq's major cities. Its land-based air defense system is designed primarily to protect its major urban areas, and key firing units could be relocated to create even greater problems in striking them without hitting civilians or producing collateral damage. Iraq would not need to deny the United States air supremacy throughout most of Iraq, but would instead need to be able to degrade the U.S. ability to operate over urban areas. This would allow it to keep most radars off most of the time and "pop on" sporadically to fire at U.S. and allied aircraft that would have to operate in more or less predictable areas.

How Much U.S. Support Is Enough?
Strengths of U.S. Strike/Attack Air and Missile Power

Another uncertainty is the level of U.S. strike attack forces that would be needed relative to a given ground component and their effectiveness against different Iraqi tactics in different scenarios.

No one can dismiss the potential impact of new strike/attack and ISR tactics and technologies on any fighting in Iraq. According to General Tommy Franks, the United States had flown an average of 200 sorties a day in Afghanistan by early February 2002, versus 3,000 a day in Desert Storm. It was, however, able to hit roughly the same number of targets per day as in Desert Storm.[41] General Franks stated that the United States needed an average of 10 aircraft to take out a target in Desert Storm; a single aircraft could often take out two targets during the fighting in Afghanistan. There also was much greater surge capability to use precision weapons against a major array of targets. In one case, the United States fired roughly 100 JDAMs in a 20-minute period.[42]

---

41. *Aerospace Daily*, February 20, 2002; General Tommy Franks, testimony to the Senate Armed Services on February 5, 2002. http://www.centcom.mil/news/transcripts/General%20Franks%20Testimony%205Feb02.htm.

42. *Aerospace Daily*, February 20, 2002; General Tommy Franks, testimony to the Senate Armed Services on February 5, 2002. http://www.centcom.mil/news/transcripts/General%20Franks%20Testimony%205Feb02.htm.

Part of the ongoing shift toward the use of precision weapons is indicated by the fact that some 6,700 of the 12,000 air weapons the United States dropped by December 7, 2001, were precision-guided—that is, 56 percent of all weapons dropped. Later estimates indicate that roughly 10,000 weapons were precision weapons out of a total of 18,000 dropped by early February—or still 56 percent. This compares with 35 percent of the 24,000 weapons dropped during the Kosovo campaign in 1999.[43] It is also worth noting that the ability to correct the dispersal of unguided submunitions for wind and greatly improved navigation and targeting capabilities also made the delivery of unguided weapons far more precise than it had been in the past.

The United States not only placed added reliance on precision-guided weapons in Afghanistan, it exploited the new abilities of U.S. forces: to draw on greatly enhanced real-time satellite, U-2, JSTARS, Rivet Joint, and UAV data on the movements of enemy and friendly forces; to target enemy forces with high precision in real time even as they were engaged by Afghan ground forces; to communicate this targeting data to U.S. bombers and strike fighters; to use the data to conduct precision strikes with both precision-guided weapons and area ordnance and then, at least partially, assess damage as well as retarget and restrike almost immediately. The United States was able to "close the loop" in conducting air and missile strikes in near real time. It was an impressive further development of techniques that owe their origins to the use of spotter aircraft and kill boxes in the Gulf War and were significantly further developed in Kosovo.

A number of the tactical encounters between U.S. and Al Qaeda forces have shown that airpower can be far more effective and responsive in close support missions and for precision weapons to act as a partial substitute for artillery under conditions where the enemy does not have high-quality short-range air defenses or large numbers of heavy weapons. A combination of fixed and rotary wing aircraft performed such missions well during the fighting at Tora Bora. Airpower and proper ISR-land-air asset management can substitute for armor and artillery in some engagements.

How Much U.S. Support Is Enough?
Limits and Key Uncertainties Affecting the Iraqi Response

It is dangerous to overgeneralize on the basis of U.S. success in recent fighting, however, because much of that success depended on rapidly achieving near-total air supremacy and U.S.-allied ability to engage enemy ground forces in ways where they could make only limited or no use of their armor or artillery against U.S. and allied forces—aside from local allies and proxies. If the U.S. air component is too light, U.S. and allied forces might have had the time to spend several weeks winning air superiority and carrying out the SEAD mission. The ground component would

---

43. General Tommy Franks, testimony to the Senate Armed Services on February 5, 2002. http://www.centcom.mil/news/transcripts/General%20Franks%20Testimony%205Feb02.htm; Bryan Bender, Kim Burger, and Andrew Koch, "Afghanistan: First Lessons," *Jane's Defense Weekly*, December 19, 2001, p. 20; *New York Times*, February 8, 2002, p. A-14, and *Philadelphia Inquirer*, February 12, 2002, p. 1.

then need more support from attack helicopters and gunships and would have to be equipped with substantially more mobile artillery and armor.

It is all too easy to assert that airpower can be decisive while sitting in an arm chair, but sending light forces against heavy forces presents major risks, and ongoing improvements in U.S. strike/attack capability do not allow limited amounts of airpower to perform miracles or airpower to be decisive in many types of close engagements.

In broad terms, the lighter the opposition (and U.S./allied) ground forces, the heavier the U.S. air and ISR element must be. However, there are no precedents for precisely estimating the required force ratios. Furthermore, the more intense the air campaign, the more precision munitions and advanced area munitions will be needed, and munitions and ISR asset scarcity could become an issue in some cases.

This makes it dangerous to count on limited or moderate amounts of U.S. airpower and predictions of what levels of U.S./allied air forces would be required over what time. It is equally difficult to determine what kind of ISR and targeting assets would be needed (and there are serious limits on many of the assets involved, and substantial numbers are tied up in Afghanistan) and how this would affect the assets available for the strike/attack mission.

Iraqi ground tactics may be able to make a major difference. Open desert operations would make Iraqi forces very vulnerable. Attacking Iraqi forces located in built-up and urban areas, sheltering in civil populations, and making extensive use of deception and decoys would be far more difficult. U.S. contingency needs for airpower and ISR assets could also escalate rapidly in a matter of hours if a U.S., allied, or opposition force should get into serious trouble in a land engagement and an Iraqi force closed determinedly and pressed the attack.

Since the beginning of U.S. military action in World War II, the U.S. military also has made a long, consistent, and historic effort of exaggerating its targeting, strike, and battle damage capabilities, of defining failure and partial success as effectiveness, and of being unable to accurately estimate civilian casualties and collateral damage.

Although General Franks has testified to the Senate Armed Services Committee that the United States needed an average of 10 aircraft to take out a target in Desert Storm, but a single aircraft could often take out two targets during the fighting in Afghanistan, it seems virtually certain that these figures will ultimately prove to be just as unrealistic as the initial battle damage claims made in the Gulf War, Desert Fox, and Kosovo.[44]

To be blunt, the U.S. military services and intelligence community simply do not yet have a credible battle damage assessment (BDA) capability against most types of targets, and they greatly compound their assessment problems by preventing operations analysis teams from entering the theater during combat. The United States has made use of an ever-changing set of rules that transform vague and inadequate damage indicators into detailed estimates by category and type. The rules

---

44. *Aerospace Daily*, February 20, 2002; General Tommy Franks, testimony to the Senate Armed Services on February 5, 2002. http://www.centcom.mil/news/transcripts/General%20Franks%20Testimony%205Feb02.htm.

and methods used in BDA have only crude analytic controls and cannot survive simple review methods like blind testing. Guesstimates rely heavily on imagery that cannot look inside buildings and shelters, often cannot tell whether a weapon was inactive or had already been damaged by other kinds of fire, and is essentially worthless in estimating infantry and human casualties.

U.S. ability to characterize sheltered and closed-in targets remains weak, as does its ability to assess and strike at hardened targets. This remains a major problem in the case of nations, like Iraq and Iran, that make extensive use of such facilities, but it is important to note that U.S. sensors and teams on the ground never succeeded in characterizing many much simpler Taliban and Al Qaeda facilities like caves. For example, the Navy SEAL team that explored the cave complex at Zhawar Kili in February had no idea that it would turn out to be the largest complex yet uncovered and had to physically enter the area to determine that the U.S. air strikes on the facility had had little or no effect and left large stocks of supplies intact.[45]

The United States has better ability to assess physical damage to surface buildings, but limited ability to assess damage to their contents. Its ability to assess functional damage to complex systems like land-based air defense systems and the resulting degree of degradation in their operational capabilities is also generally weak. The United States had major problems in these areas in the Gulf War, in Kosovo, and in 10 years of strikes against the Iraqi air defense system. It had—and still has—major problems in locating key targets, like the leadership of hostile powers or the facilities and forces related to weapons of mass destruction.

Iraq poses a particularly serious challenge in terms of efforts to suppress and destroy missiles and CBRN weapons. More broadly, the ability to reliably perform battle damage assessment remains a weak link in the U.S. ability to "close the loop" even in dealing with conventional military targets like armor, major weapons, depots, and infantry. For all the U.S. successes in Afghanistan, it is yet another warning that "closing the loop" and many other potential advantages of the "revolution in military affairs" requires far better strategic assessment and intelligence capability to determine the nature and importance of targets, better ways to assess their strategic impact and the impact of striking them, and an honest admission by the U.S. military services and intelligence community that its battle damage assessment methods are crude and inadequate, if not actively intellectually dishonest.

The Nation-building Problem

The "opposition ground force" option also presents the most risks in terms of nation building. With or without a successful decapitation strike on Saddam and those around him, it presents the problem that airpower cannot occupy populated areas or prevent some general or more political warlord from trying to take power. The one thing Iraq's weak and divided opposition elements have in common is their lack of real-world political power and popularity inside Iraq, and even if some "coalition of the impotent" could be imposed initially on Iraq from the outside, it is doubtful that it would last.

---

45. *Washington Post*, February 16, 2002, p. A-27.

The argument that "anyone would be better than Saddam" is tempting, but using military force to create a political vacuum in the Gulf could simply end in replacing "Saddam A" with "Saddam B" and creating a quieter and more subtle militarist that still proliferated, had military ambitions, and gave economic development limited priority. It also might do little to create a truly national government and deal with Iraq's ethnic and religious problems.

The High Cost of Failure

There also are serious risks to the United States and its allies in executing any option that ends in failure, and this could come from over-reliance on the Iraqi opposition with only limited U.S. military capability in place around Iraq. The cost of failure would be high:

- It would be a massive propaganda victory for Saddam Hussein and would largely discredit efforts to mount a larger-scale follow-on operation in Turkey, the Gulf, and the Middle East.

- There would be no way to decisively protect those involved in the attempt on Saddam Hussein's regime. A "Bay of Kurdistan" or "Bay of Basra" would probably be even more costly for those involved than the "Bay of Pigs."

- International support for UN sanctions and inspections could be gravely undermined or vanish.

- The security of the Kurdish enclave would at least be at risk.

- The fact that the outside opposition is so heavily penetrated by Iraqi intelligence, as internal opposition elements may also be, could lead to Iraq's carrying out its own decapitation strikes on the leaders of the opposition.

- It seems doubtful that the U.S. military presence would be large enough to provide both the needed air effort to overthrow Saddam and suppress any use of CBRN weapons, and a weak assault on the Iraqi regime is the one where Iraq might gain most by firing missiles or CBRN weapons on Israel in an attempt to try to win the support of other Arab states and possibly even drag them into the conflict.

- The U.S. presence on the ground would be far too limited to shape the future structure of Iraq, limit any civil fighting or Kurdish and Shi'ite separatism, and ensure the deterrence of Iranian adventures in southern Iraq.

- Regardless of the leader that initially replaces Saddam, if such an effort was successful, it seems likely that some form of Iraqi strong man would rapidly emerge, possibly from within the military. "Saddam A" might be replaced by "Saddam B."

- It is also unclear that the success of such an option would lead the successor to get rid of Iraqi CBRN and missile capabilities, given the broad spread of proliferation in the area, the growing threat from Iran, and Iraqi nationalism.

- A lingering battle, or opposition defeat, is the case most likely to have a serious destabilizing impact on the world oil market.

"Attack from the North" Option

There are other versions of an "opposition heavy" option, however, that involve less risk. One alternative would be to use a significant number of U.S. ground troops to attack from the north. This option would obviously require full Turkish and Kurdish cooperation—a political condition that does not now exist. However, if such cooperation can be obtained, this alternative would rely heavily on supporting Iraqi opposition ground forces with a major U.S. land force buildup in the Kurdish security zone. Some discussions of this option call for somewhere between 25,000 and 50,000 troops equipped with attack helicopters and some heavy armor. There are at least three airstrips in the general area in which the United States might deploy (before or during a conflict), which could be used to base combat aircraft or helicopters or receive intra-theater airlift.

In some scenarios, such a force would rely heavily on a mixture of attack helicopters and assault forces to conduct air assault operations and bypass Iraqi strong points, similar to the kind of operations the 101st Airborne conducted in Kuwait during the Gulf War. Such operations would limit Iraq's ability to take advantage of terrain and military operations in built-up areas (MOBA). It would also exploit the fact that Iraqi forces tend to be slow moving except when they move by road and make extensive use of tank transporters, and any such movements would make Iraqi forces far more vulnerable to U.S. airpower.

The U.S. ground force would lead the attack, but would still be supported by significant Kurdish and other opposition forces—which had significant additional training and equipment and a large Special Forces contingent present to assist them. They would be backed by a major U.S. air support effort, including air cover, air support, and a strategic bombing effort.

The end result is an "air-heavy, opposition heavy, U.S. ground force light" option, and Iraq would have several potential advantages in dealing with it. It would take time to build up such a group of forces, and Iraq could infiltrate and attack the Kurdish security zone, taking losses to U.S. air strikes, but potentially disrupting the U.S. buildup. Turkish and Kurdish support would be uncertain and possibly fragile owing to Iraqi political pressure. It also means attacking through Sunni areas and the cities and areas most likely to be loyal to Saddam once the attacking force advances beyond the Kurdish security zone.

Such an option could be combined with a U.S. attack from the south. This would obviously further reduce the risks involved, put far more pressure on Iraqi military capabilities, and limit the risk of U.S. failure.

U.S. Operations in a Major U.S.-led Coalition Military Effort

Larger-scale U.S. military intervention could take on a number of different forms, and once again, there is no magic number of forces or troops that would be necessary. Two different sets of variables are involved in making a dynamic net assessment. One deals with the options open to a U.S.-led coalition, the other with the options open to Iraq.

First, the United States can almost certainly win a conventional struggle to overthrow Saddam Hussein's regime. The issue is not so much the ability to win, but just how much force is necessary, the speed and decisiveness with which the United States does win, and the resulting political and military costs. Civilian casualties and collateral damage will be obvious problems, but so will the ability to occupy Iraq in ways that ensure its stability and lay the groundwork for effective nation building.

A U.S.-led coalition can take many different forms and can attack Iraq in a number of different ways. For example, a U.S. attack does not need to begin with a long buildup in the region in a form where *all* ground forces are in place before the attack begins. In short, the United States can begin with a paralyzing air assault and limited ground forces in place and reinforce with follow-on forces—or it can repeat the Gulf War experience of building up decisive force before combat begins. Both options have different strengths and weaknesses, and the United States has an obvious incentive to deceive Iraq as much as possible as to which option it will execute and just how much coalition support it does or does not have. War by "leak" does not have to mean war by accurate "leak."

In broad terms, however, the United States seems to have two major options for a major land-air intervention in Iraq—a "coalition heavy" or "coalition light" strategy.

"Coalition Heavy" Strategy

A "coalition heavy" strategy would involve Turkey, Kuwait, Qatar, and possibly Saudi Arabia—giving the U.S. extensive depth and scale for air options and the ability to vary its axis of attack(s) and strike from the west directly at the center of the Iraqi's regimes main bases of power, plus make maximum use of attack helicopters, air mobility, and the rapid creation of helicopter and Special Forces bases deep inside Iraq.[46] The role of Saudi Arabia is unclear, but most press reports seem to indicate that the United States would at least seek the ability to use Saudi airspace and would like to use the air command center in Riyadh and Prince Sultan Air Base—although it is planning to create an alternative at the Al Udeid air base in Qatar.

---

46.   A variation of this option is described in Eric Schmitt, "U.S. Plan for Iraq Is Said to Include Attack on Three Sides," *New York Times*, July 5, 2002, pp. A-1 and A-6. This article led the Department of Defense to launch an official investigation to try to find the person who leaked the U.S. plans referenced in the article. *New York Times*, July 21, 2002.

A massive initial air offensive would use the highly detailed strike plans the United States has refined since the Gulf War to strike at ground troops, security forces, leadership targets, communications and C^{4}I/BM targets, depots, airfields, air defenses, and selected road links to cripple and paralyze Iraq's forces while suppressing its ability to use weapons of mass destruction. Land-based airpower would be supported by extensive use of sea-based air and missile power, and covert operations might be used to strike at Iraqi CBRN and missile targets and at selected leadership targets.

The United States would use a mix of heavy and light ground forces, plus attack and assault helicopters attacking along several different axes. The exact mix of such a U.S. Army/U.S. Marine/coalition ground force is unclear, and the U.S. Army might well choose to assemble the contemporary equivalent of its "Stryker" forces by mixing limited amounts of heavy armor and artillery with lighter equipment in force mixes tailored to specific tactical missions. Estimates of the size of the force have ranged from three to five division equivalents of U.S. Army forces and 120,000–250,000 men up to two USMC division-sized expeditionary forces, 25,000 British troops, and 5 to 15 U.S. air wings.[47]

It is unclear, however, that anything like the highest levels of such force estimates reported in the press would be necessary even in the "coalition heavy" option and that such "leaks" are anything more than speculation. There are army officers outside the U.S. planning staffs working on this contingency who firmly believe that the U.S. Army would take a traditional approach to requesting massive ground forces and long periods of preparation in the United States and in the theater before beginning the land phase of the war. There are other U.S. officers who see the constant flood of reports requiring massive U.S. forces as part of a deception operation capitalizing on a seemingly endless media appetite for apparent leaks of war plans.

In any case, a "coalition heavy" strategy might involve the following military considerations:

Iraq would encounter serious problems in trying to defend against an attack on its cities from the west. The Gulf War showed that armor and assault helicopter forces can strike deep into Iraq from across the Saudi border and move rapidly through the desert toward points like Karabala, An Najaf, As Samawah, etc. If Jordan would support U.S. basing, the possibility would open up of a more direct thrust across the desert toward Ar Ramadi. There are substantial Iraqi Army, Republican Guard, and security forces in these areas, but they would have to move into the desert for any forward engagement—where they would be vulnerable to U.S. airpower—or try to use cities and the water barriers formed by lakes and the Euphrates as defensive positions. In doing so, they would risk being bypassed and could still be subjected to precision air attack.

Iraq would be better positioned to defend against a direct attack north from Kuwait toward Al Basrah and Az Zubayr and then north along the roads next to the Euphrates, Nahr al Gharraf, and Tigris toward Karbala, Al Kut, and then Baghdad.

---

47. *Daily Telegraph* (London), July 12, 2002. p. 1; UPI.com, July 12, 2002; Stratfor.com, July 10, 2002.

There are significant water barriers and urban areas that would aid Iraq in its defense, and it has significant forces in the area.

At the same time, U.S. armored and helicopter forces would have superior mobility, and U.S. airpower could cut Iraqi lines of communication and bridges and sometimes isolate Iraqi forces. Some popular uprisings might take place in Iraqi Shi'ite towns and cities, and the road net north from Kuwait is excellent.

Driving south from Turkey would involve mountain warfare at least until U.S. and allied forces reached the outskirts of Mosul, but there are several major roads south toward Bayji/Tikrit and Baghdad. Once again, Iraqi forces would be slower to maneuver, vulnerable to precision air attack, and subject to bypassing and isolation by combinations of U.S. helicopter and assault forces. Such an attack would have to drive through Sunni areas that are likely to prove most loyal to the regime, but this *could* allow a major advance from the north to seize Tikrit and have a major political impact on Iraqi morale and resolve under best-case conditions.

The United States does not have to conquer Iraq, merely isolate and defeat Saddam. The regime may not be fragile enough to produce uprisings and mass defections, but few are likely to rush in to rescue it. If the United States thrusts directly toward Baghdad, or any other central refuge for the regime, it might well be able to largely ignore the rest of Iraq. Although the United States cannot count on the collapse of the Iraqi armed forces, Saddam cannot count on their aggressive loyalty and willingness to counterattack.

"Coalition Light" or "Inside Out" Strategy

A "coalition light" or "inside out" strategy would rely on land forces staging out of Kuwait and some of the other smaller Gulf states, plus possible untried vertical envelopment, amphibious, and over-the-beach buildups. It could rely on less overt Turkish cooperation, but would involve U.S. ability to conduct air operations from Turkey—at least until a forward base(s) could be seized, secured, and made operational in Iraq. The United States might base air operations out of Bahrain, Qatar, the UAE, and Oman without active support from Saudi Arabia.

The key factor shaping such an operation would be the ability to strike at the core of Saddam Hussein's regime in areas like Baghdad and Tikrit—and bypass the largely Shi'ite areas and Iraqi land units whose movement could be paralyzed by U.S. airpower. It would use a combination of four to five heavy brigades, light divisions with attack and troop-carrying helicopters, and massive amounts of U.S. airpower to defeat Iraqi resistance at the center, while paralyzing the movement of other Iraqi forces. Such an option might require some 40,000 to 90,000 men, but the key would be to establish air superiority on day one and begin a massive air campaign immediately against all Iraqi targets—paralyzing further movement, buildup, and dispersals; suppressing Iraqi CBRN forces; and degrading communications and resupply. It would be the weight of airpower, armor, and attack and assault helicopters that would determine the success—not the number of men.

The main limitations in this approach would be the need to avoid striking (1) along a largely predictable axis and (2) under conditions where U.S. and British forces have limited ability to use air mobility and have to advance through an area with significant population and water barriers. The Kuwaiti border is long enough, however, so that it is possible that the United States could still mount an attack on Iraq from the west using a line of advance across the Wadi al Batin or moving toward Al Bussayyah.

U.S. willingness to strike decisively at Iraq's infrastructure, in spite of the political backlash and nation-building problems this raises, will be an issue in all attack scenarios. The willingness to hit hard enough to halt ground movement, create water barriers, limit Iraq's ability to move by road, and make it difficult to use towns and cities as sanctuaries is critical to U.S. ability to exploit Iraq's relatively slow maneuver capability and heavy dependence on roads, tank transporters, and flooding supplies forward to compensate for the inadequacies of its logistic system. It is also critical to making use of the shock power of air and missile strikes rather than simply relying on damage and attrition, and such shock power is often at least as important as casualties and material damage.

Much would depend on U.S. willingness to use new tactics to take advantage of attack helicopters and heliborne assault forces. The 101st Airborne demonstrated during the Gulf War that large mixes of attack helicopters and heliborne assault forces can rapidly stage forward and can engage even heavy armored forces using missiles like the Hellfire. These missions were part of a massive armored advance during the Gulf War and took place against an enemy already in retreat. Some argue, however, that U.S. airpower can now secure forward staging bases against an Iraqi armored advance and, even if U.S. forces were forced to retreat and regroup, that in the process of attacking such U.S. helicopter and heliborne assault-force staging bases, the Iraqi armor would become so exposed to U.S. air strikes that they would take unacceptable casualties.

The U.S. Army is exploring a somewhat similar option for using armored forces. Traditionally, armored advances require extensive ground troops to secure their flanks. The army is experimenting, however, with the idea of sending armored or mechanized thrusts directly at critical objectives and using airpower to secure the flanks of such forces, halt counterattacks, and allow the advancing force to bypass enemy strong points. Only professional military officers can assess the cost-benefits of such operations in Iraq, but they could significantly reduce the level of U.S. forces required.

Much also depends on U.S. Army willingness to develop new mixes of armor and light mechanized forces similar to the new Stryker or interim combat brigade teams it is developing as an interim approach to the "Army of the future." Altering this mix could allow the United States to use far fewer heavy tanks, other armored vehicles, and artillery weapons and still preserve a core of advanced heavy forces. In fact, such a mix may be essential even in the near term since the army's efforts to develop lighter armored combat vehicles have so far failed to solve the problem of size, and lift will be "cubic capacity" rather than weight-limited once they are deployed.

The United States would benefit in all contingencies from having time to prepare some aspects of the battlefield. The United States has limited ISR assets, and such assets can greatly improve the effectiveness of a given amount of U.S. airpower as well as support U.S. and allied ground forces. The United States has shortfalls in some categories in munitions and is still expanding its pre-positioning and support facilities in the smaller southern Gulf states. Full access to Bahrain, Kuwait, Oman, Qatar, and the UAE would be critical in such a contingency, particularly to expanded air facilities in Bahrain, Kuwait, and Qatar such as the Al Udeid Air Base.

Amphibious and Vertical Envelopment Operations

An amphibious attack is technically possible. An over-the-beach operation only makes sense except as a feint, given the mix of terrain and water barriers involved and the relatively poor strategic position offered by deploying U.S. forces on Iraq's small coastline. However, U.S. Marine forces might be used in a heliborne vertical envelopment to attack key Iraqi facilities in the south that did not have heavy armor and firepower. They could also be combined with the Special Forces of other services, which could make use of amphibious ships as joint "lily pads."

The Al Basrah, An Nasiriyah, and Al Amarah areas would present problems for Iraq if the United States even feinted against such cities. The Iraqi regime could not count on Shi'ite loyalty, and it would lack the air combat and survivable heliborne mobility to counter U.S. assault helicopter movements. This could mean either abandoning key cities in the south or tying down significant Iraqi ground troops out of the relatively limited number of high-quality divisions the regime can count on.

The Value of Coalition Military Support

Much will depend on U.S. ability to obtain political, military, and basing support from key regional powers, like Turkey and Saudi Arabia, as well as the support of the smaller Gulf states and world opinion. The fact that the United States might be able to destroy Saddam's regime with minimum foreign basing and coalition support is scarcely an incentive to attack Iraq in this way, and a U.S. effort to attack Saddam's regime without broad regional support would severely limit the flexibility and depth of the U.S. air and land attack, provide the Iraqi regime with major propaganda advantages, and present major problems in effective postwar nation building.

Depths of land and air operations are important and depend on allied support. A two-front U.S.-allied air operation with ample depth for refueling, basing, staging task groups, and flying ISR assets is a major advantage, but it requires access to Turkey and either Saudi Arabia or all of the smaller Gulf states. A multiple-axis advance in the south is far easier with forces in Saudi Arabia, and advancing from both the north and south would put far more pressure on Iraqi forces, as well as provide more political control.

Iraq does have large numbers of civilian and military air bases, some of them comparatively isolated in desert areas or away from built-up areas. The seizure of bases in Iraq could substitute for reliance on allies, allow the rapid staging of U.S. attack helicopter and assault forces, and confront Iraq with either having to attack under conditions where its forces would become more vulnerable to U.S. airpower or see a major, sudden improvement in U.S. staging capability.

How Much U.S. Force Is Enough?

Although various analysts and journalists have quoted figures for U.S. manpower requirements, such estimates are little more than military drivel. The number of people engaged in battles had little impact on outcome as early as the U.S. civil war, and the type and quality of forces has long been critical. The U.S. Joint Staff has clearly developed a range of contingency plans to attack Iraq and overthrow Saddam Hussein's regime, although President Bush has not approved any given option. These options involve a wide range of force mixes, assumptions about coalition warfare, and methods of attack. The United States can alter the mix of air and land power to stress airpower, put in significant armor and other heavy forces, and deploy different mixes of air assault and attack helicopter forces.

"Decisive force" would probably have to involve the early commitment of at least several U.S. division equivalents, including heavy armored forces and major air assault and attack helicopter forces, several wings of U.S. combat aircraft, and a mass land-air support effort involving very substantial C^4I/BM, ISR, electronic warfare (EW), and dedicated intelligence assets. It is also far easier to send underutilized forces home after a conflict than compensate for shortfall during a conflict.

U.S. willingness to use air and missile power decisively and to exploit what is likely to be rapid air supremacy will sharply affect Iraq's ability to maneuver, reinforce, supply, and cross water barriers. It will be equally important in determining Iraq's ability to shelter in cities and use human shields and in suppressing Iraqi ability to preserve its CBRN weapons and missiles. There will, however, be obvious trade-offs in terms of civilian casualties and collateral damage, including serious potential damage to Iraq's infrastructure if the U.S. wish to isolate cities, shatter LOCs, and inflict major coercive damage on those cities and towns that become redoubts for the regime.

Even with high levels of U.S. forces, much would still depend on how rapidly the United States could suppress Iraqi surface-based air defenses in the populated areas, the level of U.S. airpower that would have to go into the SEAD mission, and the effectiveness and survivability of short and medium land-based air defenses in dealing with attack helicopters, other helicopters, and fixed-wing aircraft forced into relatively short-range engagements. The issue would not be whether the United States could succeed, but what levels of force would be required over what time, what kind of ISR and targeting assets would be needed (there are serious limits on many of the assets involved, and substantial numbers are tied up in Afghanistan), and how this would affect the assets available for the strike/attack mission.

Once again, the United States and its allies cannot predict how much strike/attack airpower will be needed to deal with a given Iraqi force in a given position. Open desert operations would make Iraqi forces very vulnerable. Attacking them in built-up and urban areas, sheltering in civil populations, would be far more difficult. Similar problems arise in trying to estimate contingency needs if a U.S., allied, or opposition force should get into serious trouble in a land engagement and an Iraqi force closed determinedly and pressed the attack. In broad terms, the lighter the ground forces, the heavier the air must be, but there are no precedents for accurately estimating the required force ratios. Furthermore, the more intense the air campaign, the more precision munitions and advanced area munitions will be needed, and scarcity could become an issue in some cases. Having sufficient ground forces to occupy large areas in Iraq will be critical to ensuring that ethnic and civil conflicts do not take place, that no Iranian-sponsored adventures occur, and that air efforts to suppress Iraq's CBRN forces can be reinforced with effective efforts on the ground. Significant Arab and Turkish support for such missions would be of major help in reducing any Iraqi nationalist reactions or religious tensions, but could not substitute for a U.S.-UK ground presence.

Factors Shaping Iraqi Operations in a Major U.S.-led Coalition Military Effort

Iraq cannot hope to win a conventional war in the face of decisive U.S. force, but it does have a wide range of options, and some might be effective in the face of inadequate U.S. and coalition force levels:

The key battle is already under way and is largely political. Iraq's best strategy is to defuse the political momentum for a major U.S. attack on Iraq and to win as much Arab support as it can. This means strengthening the political accommodation it has already reached with other Arab states—including Kuwait and Saudi Arabia—and attempting to win broad Arab political support through its support for the Palestinian cause in the Second Intifada. Some form of Iraqi accommodation in terms of resuming UN inspections is another potential option, although one that Saddam and other hard-liners in the regime are certain to be reluctant to take. Using oil wealth and control over much of the media to mobilizing popular support is another approach the regime is taking, one that both deters U.S. military action and strengthens Iraqi operational capabilities. In contrast, the United States faces the backlash from the Second Intifada, has been unable to mobilize Arab or European support for a war tied largely to the threat of proliferation, and has no smoking gun in terms of Iraqi support for terrorism.

The worst Iraqi option is to repeat the mistakes of the Gulf War and send its best forces out into the desert where they are most exposed and have the least air defense. Some counterattacks and raids may be needed, but a forward defense strategy is the one most vulnerable to U.S. military action. Similarly, digging in forward areas and the extensive use of static forces and earth barriers could be useful in defending Basra and a few critical lines of communication, but make Iraqi forces easy to bypass and outmaneuver.

A city-populated area based strategy presents the most problems for the United States in using airpower effectively and provides the most political advantages in exploiting collateral damage and civilian casualties. It also is unlikely to lead to uprisings or opposition action as long as loyal forces are in place and willing to fight.

Iraq may be able to exploit water barriers against heavy U.S. forces, but is more likely to lose bridges and road mobility to U.S. airpower. Pre-positioning forces and supplies to defend a limited part of the country with the most loyal population and most critical cities—an urban redoubt strategy—offers more survivable flexibility than either a forward deployed or central reserve strategy. Iraq's surface-to-air missile system also supports such a strategy.

Some form of Iraqi redoubt and scorched-earth strategy is also an option. Iraq set Kuwait's oil fields on fire during the Gulf War and might well try to use the oil weapon in such a contingency. It has already talked about oil embargoes in the context of the Second Intifada, and Saddam Hussein might well see burning Iraq's oil fields and CBRN attacks on major Gulf oil fields as both a defense and form of revenge. Iraq could also combine such a strategy with falling back on a largely Shi'ite-dominated "redoubt" by using the cities and towns in north central Iraq for its defense while leaving as much of a scorched earth as possible in the areas of a U.S.-led coalition advance.

Fighting delaying actions inside urban areas offers Iraq a way of using human shields, limiting U.S. air strike capability and forcing U.S.-led coalition forces to fight on the most restricted terms. It cannot win against mobility and decisive force, but it is certain to be more effective than putting infantry in earth barriers—the "speed bump" strategy that Iraq used in the Gulf War.

Iraq is virtually certain to try to exploit civilian casualties and collateral damage as a political and media weapon and mix this with the use of deception and decoys. Saddam Hussein's regime will attempt to fight a political battle to the last.

Iraq might try to use CBRN weapons to preempt a U.S. buildup, launch on warning (LOW), or launch under attack (LUA) against key U.S. and coalition bases. He might try to use selective escalation to using remaining missiles and/or CBRN weapons to try to involve Israel in the war risks escalating the physical damage to Iraq and make maximum use of the backlash from the Second Intifada. Saddam Hussein seems to have put his missiles and CBRN forces in the hands of loyalists who might well execute an LOW, LUA, and/or desperate retaliatory option. The problem with a desperate retaliatory option is that Saddam must realize that waiting until the regime is collapsing and then conducting CBRN operations against Arab states, or conducting covert CBRN strikes against the United States when the regime is already in extremis, is far more likely to increase the severity of coalition action. He must also realize that major, highly lethal, Iraqi CBRN strikes on Israeli population centers are likely to trigger a nuclear war.

The Key Military Issue Is the Cost to the United States of Winning

Anyone who looks seriously at this list of independent variables will quickly see that it is impossible to predict whether and how the United States will use decisive force, the Iraqi response to a U.S.-led coalition, the nature of a U.S.-led coalition, how long Iraq can endure, and what strategy Iraq will actually pursue if it does use its CBRN weapons.

What does seem likely, however, is that it would take a major U.S. miscalculation about the size of the forces needed to defeat Iraq or a poorly structured and overconstrained U.S. operation to allow Iraq to ride out the U.S.-led attack through even the best combination of urban and redoubt warfare. Furthermore, most forms of extreme Iraq escalation can make things worse for both the attacker and defender, but will probably end in hurting Iraq more than the attacker.

CHAPTER 7

Conflict Termination and Nation Building

It seems doubtful that Saddam Hussein and his supporters could take to the countryside and mount any kind of major insurgent or guerrilla operation over time. Like the Taliban, they simply do not seem popular enough to survive a systematic defeat of their conventional war-fighting capability. Much of the mid- to long-term success of any U.S.-led operation will, however, depend on the ability to occupy the country with friendly forces, provide suitable peacekeeping forces, provide immediate repairs to critical infrastructure, and institute a development and economic recovery program to aid the Iraqi people.

In fact, a clear nation-building plan will be critical to obtaining the support of the Iraqi people during the war, gaining the support of Arabs and other allies, reassuring Iran, and minimizing the political costs of inevitable civilian casualties and collateral damage. It should also be clear from experience in the Balkans and Afghanistan that nation building cannot be done on the cheap and without a long-term commitment. This will be particularly true of a country that has spent nearly two decades either at war or under UN sanctions and faces massive debt and reparations payments.

Replacing Saddam Hussein's regime with a more discrete version of the same thing is not victory in any meaningful sense and may well simply leave Iraq to founder under a new military leader, one committed to continuing with proliferation and rebuilding Iraq's military strength. It would also do much to discredit U.S. military success, just as Saddam Hussein's survival after the Gulf War deprived that victory of much of its meaning. The world will also have little reason to trust and admire a United States that defeats a dictator and then abandons Iraq without creating a stable political and social structure, rule of law and human rights, basis for ethnic and sectarian cooperation, and economic development.

Unfortunately, the United States has shown in the past that it can execute military operations without any clear plan for conflict termination and nation building. The American military culture seems to believe that its responsibility ends with strategy and that grand strategy is the province of politicians and God. The American political culture—whether led by Bush or Clinton—seeks to avoid realistic planning for the true scale of the problems, costs, and timelines involved and prefers to rely on rhetoric, good intentions, and hope. A clear nation-building plan backed with the military forces necessary to implement it and strong political and economic incentives to the Iraqi people is far more likely to lead to rapid U.S. success. So is a realistic plan that balances the sensitivities of Iraqi factions and ethnic groups and that considers the strategic interests of Turkey, the Arab states around Iraq, and Iran.

The United States also needs to avoid anything approaching a "mandate" or a Weimar solution. It should be clear that the United States intends to leave as soon as it has met the needs of the Iraqi people and has brought as many neighboring states as possible into the peacekeeping and reconstruction effort. It should rely on Arab states and forces wherever possible in those cases where Iraqi forces cannot do the job. It should be prepared to immediately help reorganize and retrain Iraqi police and security forces.

Economic integrity is equally critical. The United States should make it clear that it will not exploit any aspect of its actions to win Iraqi oil or other contracts and that it will support open and competitive international bidding. It should be prepared to forgive all remaining debt and reparations owed by Iraq and use ruthless diplomatic pressure to persuade other nations to follow this example when they lack the wisdom to do so voluntarily. It must be made clear to Kuwait and Saudi Arabia that this is one contribution to any overthrow of Saddam Hussein that they must make. Only Iraqis can remake Iraq, but the international community can both help and avoid repeating past mistakes.

Iraq has many well-educated and competent administrators in spite of Saddam Hussein's regime, and a strong initial U.S. military effort can suppress "warlordism" and help create a fair balance of ethnic and sectarian interests. The United States cannot, however, rely on "spontaneous democracy" to solve its problems or a simplistic form of "democratization." Iraq cannot create a stable set of political parties and factions without time, and electing a strong man or some largely self-appointed leader quickly after Saddam's exit is not an answer. In fact, "democratization" alone begs some of the most fundamental needs of the Iraqi people. It does not protect human rights or institute a rule of law. It does not protect property and commercial operations and encourage honest outside investment. "Democratization" does not imply the equivalent of a Marshall Plan or economic reform. The United States and the world may still have to discover what nation building really should be and the best techniques to make it work, but simple-minded slogans clearly are not the answer.

Blundering into grand strategy is not a plan. At best, it is victory ending in accident, and the human costs can be all too real. Military adventures that kill U.S. troops and local allies and end in frustration are even worse, and civilian casualties and collateral damage have a moral price tag. Here, it is worthwhile to remember another quotation from the classical world, this time by Pliny the Elder: "Small boys throw stones at frogs in jest. But the frogs do not die in jest. The frogs die in earnest."

Iraqi vs. Neighboring Forces in 2002

	Iran	Iraq	Bahrain	Kuwait	Saudi Arabia**	Turkey	Jordan	Syria
Manpower								
Total active	513,000	424,000	11,000	15,500	201,500	515,100	100,240	321,000
Regular	325,000	375,000	11,000	15,500	105,500	515,100	100,240	321,000
National Guard & other	125,000	0	0	0	75,000	0	0	0
Reserve	350,000	650,000	0	23,700	20,000	378,700	35,000	354,000
Paramilitary	40,000	42,000+	10,160	5,000	15,500+	152,200	10,000	108,000
Army and guard manpower	450,000*	375,000	8,500	11,000	150,000	402,000	84,700	215,000
Regular army manpower	325,000	375,000	8,500	11,000	75,000	402,000	84,700	215,000
Reserve	350,000	650,000	0	0	20,000	258,700	30,000	280,000
Total main battle tanks***	1,565	2,200	106	385	1,055	4,205	1,058	3,500 (1,200)
Active main battle tanks	1,565	1,900	106	293	710	2,995	1,030	3,200
Active AIFV/Recce, lt. tanks	865	1,300	71	355	1,270+	3,600	85	3,285
Total APCs	590	2,400	235	151	3,440	3,643	1,130	1,600
Active APCs	550	1,800	205	111	2,630	3,480	980	1,200
ATGM launchers	75	100+	15	118	480+	943	640	6,050
Self-propelled artillery	310	150	62	68 (18)	200	668	418	450
Towed artillery	2,085	1,900	22	0	238(58)	679	113	1,630
MRLs	889+	200	9	27	60	84	0	480
Mortars	5,000	2,000+	21	78	400	2,021	700	658
SSM launchers	51	56	0	0	10	0	0	72
Light SAM launchers	?	1,100	78	0	650	897	944	4,055
AA guns	1,700	6,000	27	0	10	1,664	416	2,060
Air force manpower	30,000	30,000	1,500	2,500	20,000	60,100	15,000	40,000
Air defense manpower	15,000	17,000	0	0	16,000	0	0	60,000
Total combat aircraft	283	316	34	82	348	505	101	589
Bombers	0	6	0	0	0	0	0	0
Fighter/attack	163+	130	12	40	100	-	70	154
Fighter/interceptor	74+	180	22	14	181	-	31	310

	Iran	Iraq	Bahrain	Kuwait	Saudi Arabia	Turkey	Jordan	Syria
Recce/FGA Recce	6	5	0	0	10	59	0	14
AEW C4I/BM	1	0	0	0	5	7	0	0
MR/MPA**	5	0	0	0	0	-	0	0
OCU/COIN/CCT	0	0	0	28	14	-	0	0
Other combat trainers	35	157	0	0	50	-	0	111
Transport aircraft****	68	12	3	4	61	80		25
Tanker aircraft	4	2	0	0	16	7	0	0
Total helicopters	628	375	47	28	137	-	73	197
Armed helicopters****	104	100	40	16	21	37	20	87
Other helicopters****	524	275	7	12	116	-	53	110
Major SAM launchers	250+	400	15	84	106	92	80	648
Light SAM launchers	?	1,100	-	60	309	86	-	60
AA guns	-	6,000	-	60	340	-	-	4,000
Total naval manpower	38,000*	2,000	1,000	2,000	15,500	53,000	540	6,000
Regular navy	15,400	2,000	1,000	2,000	12,500	49,900	540	6,000
Naval guards	20,000	0	0	0	0	0	0	0
Marines	2,600	-	-	-	3,000	3,100	0	0
Major surface combatants								
Missile	3	0	3	0	8	22	0	0
Other	0	0	0	0	0	1	0	2
Patrol craft								
Missile	10	1	6	10	9	21	0	10
(Revolutionary Guards)	10	-	-	-	-	-	-	-
Other	42	5	4	0	17	28	3	8
Revolutionary Guards (boats)	40	-	-	-	-	-	-	-
Submarines	3	0	0	0	0	13	0	0
Mine vessels	7	3	0	0	7	24	0	5
Amphibious ships	9	0	0	0	0	8	0	3
Landing craft	9	-	4	2	8	59	0	4
Support ships	22	2	5	4	7	27	0	4
Naval air	2,000	-	-	-	-	-	0	0
Naval aircraft								
Fixed wing combat	5	0	0	0	0	0	0	0
MR/MPA	10	0	0	0	0	0	0	0
Armed helicopters	19	0	0	0	21	16	0	16
SAR helicopters	-	0	0	0	4	0	0	0
Mine warfare helicopters	3	0	0	0	0	0	0	0
Other helicopters	19	-	2	-	6	7	0	-

Note: Equipment in storage shown in the higher figure in parenthesis or in range. Air force totals include all helicopters, including army-operated weapons and all heavy surface-to-air missile launchers.

* Iranian total includes roughly 100,000 Revolutionary Guard actives in land forces and 20,000 in naval forces.

** Saudi totals for reserve include National Guard Tribal Levies. The total for land forces includes active National Guard equipment. These additions total 450 AIFVs, 730(1,540) APCs, and 70 towed artillery weapons.

*** Total tanks include tanks in storage or conversion.

**** Includes navy, army, National Guard, and royal flights, but not paramilitary.

Source: Adapted by Anthony H. Cordesman from interviews; IISS, *Military Balance, 2001–2002*; *Jane's Sentinel Security Assessments* and *Periscope*; and Jaffee Center for Strategic Studies, *The Military Balance in the Middle East, 2000–2001* (Tel Aviv: JCSS, 2001).

Measures of Combat Equipment Strength, 2002

Total main battle tanks in inventory

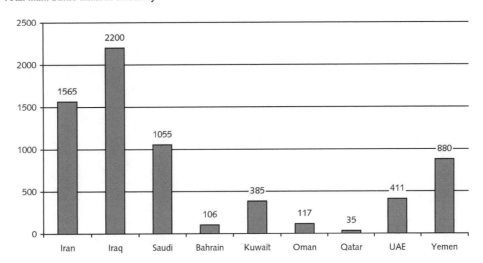

Total fixed wing combat aircraft

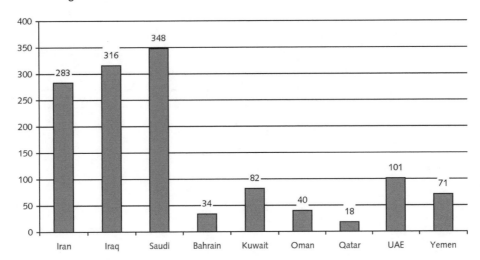

Source: Estimated by Anthony H. Cordesman using data from IISS, *Military Balance, 2001–2002,* the online edition of *Jane's Sentinel Security Assessments,* and Jane's online edition of *Periscope.*

Gulf Arms Buys by Supplier, 1987–2000

(new arms agreements in current U.S.$millions)

Buyer Country	Supplier Country						Total
	United States	Russia	China	Major West European	Other European	All Others	
Iran							
1987-1990	0	3,500	2,300	200	1,200	1,600	8,800
1991-1994	0	200	200	100	100	600	1,200
1995-1998	0	200	800	0	300	100	1,400
1996-1999	0	200	800	0	100	0	1,100
1997-2000	0	300	600	100	100	200	1,300
Iraq							
1987-1990	0	300	700	500	500	1,000	3,000
1991-1994	0	0	0	0	0	0	0
1995-1998	0	0	0	0	0	0	0
1996-1999	0	0	0	0	0	0	0
1997-2000	0	0	0	0	0	0	0
Bahrain							
1987-1990	300	0	0	0	0	0	300
1991-1994	200	0	0	0	0	0	200
1995-1998	500	0	0	0	0	0	500
1996-1999	500	0	0	0	0	0	500
1997-2000	700	0	0	0	0	0	700
Kuwait							
1987-1990	2,500	200	0	200	200	200	3,300
1991-1994	3,500	800	0	1,800	0	100	6,200
1995-1998	900	0	200	700	100	0	1,900
1996-1999	800	0	200	100	0	0	1,100
1997-2000	500	0	200	0	0	0	700
Oman							
1987-1990	100	0	0	600	0	0	700
1991-1994	0	0	0	500	0	100	600
1995-1998	0	0	0	300	100	100	500
1996-1999	0	0	0	300	100	0	400
1997-2000	0	0	0	300	100	0	400